Experiences of Adults Following an Autism Diagnosis

Kristien Hens • Raymond Langenberg

Experiences of Adults Following an Autism Diagnosis

palgrave
macmillan

Kristien Hens
Department of Philosophy
University of Antwerp
Antwerp, Belgium

Raymond Langenberg
Diversity - Campus Gelbergen
Hoeleden, Belgium

ISBN 978-3-319-97972-4   ISBN 978-3-319-97973-1   (eBook)
https://doi.org/10.1007/978-3-319-97973-1

Library of Congress Control Number: 2018951792

© The Editor(s) (if applicable) and The Author(s), under exclusive license to Springer Nature Switzerland AG 2018
This work is subject to copyright. All rights are solely and exclusively licensed by the Publisher, whether the whole or part of the material is concerned, specifically the rights of translation, reprinting, reuse of illustrations, recitation, broadcasting, reproduction on microfilms or in any other physical way, and transmission or information storage and retrieval, electronic adaptation, computer software, or by similar or dissimilar methodology now known or hereafter developed.
The use of general descriptive names, registered names, trademarks, service marks, etc. in this publication does not imply, even in the absence of a specific statement, that such names are exempt from the relevant protective laws and regulations and therefore free for general use.
The publisher, the authors and the editors are safe to assume that the advice and information in this book are believed to be true and accurate at the date of publication. Neither the publisher nor the authors or the editors give a warranty, express or implied, with respect to the material contained herein or for any errors or omissions that may have been made. The publisher remains neutral with regard to jurisdictional claims in published maps and institutional affiliations.

Cover Pattern © Melisa Hasan

This Palgrave Pivot imprint is published by the registered company Springer Nature Switzerland AG
The registered company address is: Gewerbestrasse 11, 6330 Cham, Switzerland

Acknowledgements

The publication of this book would not have been possible without the support and feedback of many. First and foremost, we would like to thank our conversation partners for their openness and their willingness to participate in the interviews. Both the people of Campus Gelbergen and the people of Autism Ethics Network have provided valuable feedback on presentations we did of the work in progress. In thankful memory of Leo Beyers, Raymond Langenberg would like to emphasise the importance of the Communication Analysis conversations, which have been of great importance to him in exploring his qualities on a social and interpersonal level. Special thanks to Suzan Langenberg for her stimulating role to study communication and search for means of expression and phrasings to enable the communication of the unsayable. We would also like to thank the anonymous reviewers, both in Dutch and in English, for their constructive remarks. We thank Fleur Beyers for her excellent editing job, Chelsea Oostdijk for her fantastic job on the English translation and Robert Borremans, who—together with Kristien Hens—was responsible for transcribing the interviews.

About the Drawings

When you are unable to directly express what is on your mind, it is difficult to participate in events with other people. Not that you easily become aware of this, because there are all sorts of patterns (escape routes) in communication to let that pass unnoticed.

There are patterns of agreements where you do something for someone else. This is already a dangerous area, however, because when this becomes too intellectual, things can go wrong. Collecting things for someone else, or fetching something, or offering something, is relatively safe. The reciprocity of these kinds of patterns is also surmountable. But when you make an agreement about a text or about a document that must be written or an inventory that must be drawn up, it is imperative that you clearly understand exactly what it is you have agreed upon. Most of the time, having exactly the same understanding of an agreement can be a source of misunderstandings. On top of that, a certain imbalance may arise in the immediate contact because it is often the other who says what he wants, chooses or thinks.

In the Communication Analysis conversations with Leo Beyers—which we had on a weekly basis for a period of 20 years—he suggested I make a drawing about how I thought it is to communicate with me and how I thought it was going.

So this was said and done.

With this, a broader world came within reach. It became possible for me to no longer merely react, and no longer hide and get trapped in guesses about what I thought the other expected from me. I could learn to speak about what I had mapped out and think about why I drew it like that, the way I depicted it.

It became possible to speak about that which I had not yet developed an awareness of, or whereof I was not capable in the previous period. Because I kept throwing something in between that always, in one way or another, had something to do with trying to meet expectations.

Initially, my drawings were very rudimentary patterns, lines and smileys I used to outline the course of a conversation. Later on, I also added possible thoughts, ideas and responses to the drawings. Similar to the example of 'the helping thoughts' of BartDelam,[1] I also assessed the possible responses to an event.

I discovered that a line on a piece of paper can also express something, and slowly but steadily I started to work more with impressions. There was a period that the drawings I had made in my most difficult moments of despair, self-criticism, insecurity and not knowing evoked the most recognition and left the biggest impression on others. The drawings from this publication came into being while working on the interviews with the people who participated in this book. Profoundly struck by the seriousness and depth of the conversations, I was only able to express the effect this had on me by drawing it. I have been able to do the textual processing of the interviews and our research mostly in dialogue with Kristien Hens, but also with others who have conversed with me about this study.

Raymond Langenberg

---

[1] See Chap. 5 (Autism as a Way to Hold Your Own) and Appendix (The Helping Thoughts of BartDelam).

Contents

1 Introduction 1

2 Being 'Different' 21

3 Perspectives on Suffering 43

4 The Experience of Being Tested 61

5 Autism as a Way to Hold Your Own 79

6 The (In)ability to Self-Reflect 95

7 To Challenge or to Accept 105

8 Perspectives on the Future 117

9 Afterthoughts 129

Appendix: The Helping Thoughts of BartDelam 137

Glossary 143

Bibliography 147

Index 153

LIST OF TABLES

Table 1.1   Overview of participants   13
Table 1.2   Interview schedule   15

CHAPTER 1

Introduction

Abstract The authors are Kristien Hens (University Professor in Ethics) and Raymond Langenberg (Management Consultant). The latter is writing from his own experience of receiving and coming to terms with a diagnosis of Asperger's syndrome. In this introduction, they start by exploring different meanings of autism, after which they provide an outline of the methodology they used for this project.

Keywords Autism • Dimensions • Definition • Phenomenology • Experience

What does it mean to feel different? How does it feel to be diagnosed with autism as an adult? Although there are libraries filled with books that explain autism based on biological or cognitive models, these two questions have not yet been thoroughly investigated. Moreover, for a long time, autism was considered to be a children's disorder, neglecting the perspective of adults with the diagnosis.

The idea to further research this perspective was born in August 2015 when two researchers met at the *29th European Conference on Philosophy of Medicine and Health Care* in Ghent, Belgium: Kristien Hens, lecturer at the University of Antwerp, who had at that time just finished a short project on genetics and autism, and Raymond Langenberg, co-initiator of the independent think tank Campus Gelbergen, who, inspired by his own diagnosis of Asperger's, was working on his own research project.

Kristien Hens' project was based on bio-ethical questions such as "should all children with a diagnosis of autism be genetically tested?", "what is the purpose of fundamental research on the genetics of autism?" and "is it justified that genetic knowledge about autism is being used for reproductive goals such as embryo selection or prenatal diagnosis?" At an early stage of her research, it already became clear that these questions were fundamentally insoluble, at least, when using prevailing and conventional theories on autism. After all, the answer to these questions depends on the perspective on autism: is it a disease? A behaviour? Or could it in certain cases perhaps just be a different way of thinking, a way that could possibly also have its benefits? Up until now, the available academic literature predominantly regards autism from a medical perspective: autism is a disorder that should be explained and possibly also cured or prevented. Few studies have tried to understand what having a diagnosis of autism actually *means*.

Raymond Langenberg is partner in Belgian training and consultancy company Diversity, as well as a researcher with Campus Gelbergen, an independent think tank and research institute that organises lectures and debates between practitioners and theorists and publishes books on business, philosophy and societal issues (*Cahiers Campus Gelbergen*). The people behind Campus Gelbergen have extensive experience with Communication Analysis. Communication Analysis is a research practice where the analyst, confronted with a co-researcher, tries to analyse his or her share in the interaction with the other. Actor, director and later philosopher Leo Beyers developed this practice analysis in the mid-1980s[1] from a dramaturgical perspective. Precisely from the awareness that every expert has an object relation to that which he wants to study, Beyers states that this represents just *one* kind of knowing: the knowing *about* and thinking *about*. Communication Analysis, however, studies the practice of knowing that originates from *the subject itself* (the analyst), in counter-conduct[2] with the other, the other subject (the associate). The critical counter-conduct herein is aimed at "(...) understanding myself (...) understanding, changing myself gradually during the conversation, the experience, through and with the other recognising him as *an other that changes me.*"[3] This can also be applied to the context of autism. Analysing

---

[1] Beyers (2014, pp. 7–12).
[2] See Michel Foucault's concept *counter-conduct*, resistance against ruling discourse.
[3] Idem. p. 18.

how autistic people handle social situations may be more productive than holding on to a diagnosis that says that social situations can cause problems and people to withdraw. In Beyers' Communication Analysis, it is precisely these situations that are examined and engaged with in order to determine and register what someone—for instance with a diagnosis of autism—perceives or observes. This takes experience, orientation, thought, logic and behaviours into account that were developed by this someone in order to survive (coping behaviour). Current criticism of all these aspects also opens up a space of discovery and selection where meaning can be created and exchanged and lifted to a social level of interaction. This usually leads to a deeper contact and a more profound conversation for both of the conversation partners. The interviews that are the common thread within this study, represent these reflections that transcend the simple 'taking someone into account'.

From his practice as an andragogue (social sciences), Raymond Langenberg is working on a longitudinal study of the meaning of diagnostics. In this study, he explores how self-reflection, that moves beyond a certain dysfunctioning, can be made possible, as it is a necessity in order to find your bearings in life, work and thought. Langenberg was diagnosed with Asperger's himself 14 years before the beginning of the project and is also from this perspective interested in the question of the meaning of diagnostics.

Before giving an outline of our study, we would like to propose a few layers of meaning of the concept of autism. We understand that to some readers, this may seem a complex theoretical treatise or a repetition of what is already known about autism. We have nevertheless decided to include this in this book because it could serve as an important frame of reference for people who are less informed about the subject. Apart from this specific framework, the reader will notice that this book leaves the perspective of *writing about* the phenomenon and continues to *write from* the experience and perception of the interviewees.

Autism is first and foremost a concept from *clinical practice*. When people have autism, or are diagnosed with autism, it means that they meet certain *behavioural criteria*. This means that the diagnosis is based on an observation of behaviour and that this behaviour must have such an effect on the diagnosed person that he or she dysfunctions considerably. Which diagnostic manual is used for the diagnosis depends on where you are diagnosed, and whether—in that place and time—a newer version of testing instruments has already been accepted as a formal diagnostic device.

In this context, it is important to note that throughout the years, autism has gained a broader meaning in diagnostics. In the mid-1900s, Leo Kanner already wrote about 11 children who supposedly had an affective disorder, an *autistic aloneness*.[4] With the various revisions of the *Diagnostic and Statistical Manual of Mental Disorders* (DSM), the definition of autism developed into *a spectrum of behaviours*, in the fifth edition characterised by problems with communication and social kills on the one hand, and repetitive behaviours on the other hand.[5] At the time the interviews for this book were being held (2016), social security in the Netherlands still used DSM-IV as a guideline, whereas in Belgium, DSM-5 was already applicable.[6] The most important difference between DSM-IV and DSM-5 with respect to autism is that the most recent version (a) speaks of a dyad of persistent deficits in social communication and social interaction and (b) speaks of restrictive and repetitive patterns of behaviour, interests, or activities.[7] In DSM-IV, this was still regarded as a triad, and communication and social interaction were regarded separately. Another revision in DSM-5 is the addition of the former diagnoses of the syndrome of Asperger and *Pervasive Developmental Disorder—Not Otherwise Specified* (PDD-NOS) to 'Autism Spectrum Disorder'. Furthermore, a multidimensional approach of the diagnosis was tried: various people with a diagnosis of autism can exhibit more or less of a certain trait. Nevertheless, the diagnosis is still categorical: you either have autism or you do not. You cannot just be a little autistic. The aspect of dysfunctioning—which is conditional to the diagnosis—is also important. After all, the extent to which someone dysfunctions can depend on a few intrinsic traits of the individual. For instance: your IQ can offer protection, but it can also exaggerate certain symptoms, and the extent to which you suffer from sensory overstimulation can depend on how your brain is put together and so on. However, it also depends very much on the context. If the DSM-5 criteria are followed strictly, someone who meets these criteria will be able to live with them and accept their existence in their daily life, but he or she will not necessarily qualify for the actual diagnosis of autism. Or—in the context of academic research—a population could be screened for autistic

[4] Kanner (1968).
[5] See DSM-5. p. 50.
[6] From January 1, 2017, The Netherlands also uses the DSM-5 as a guideline for diagnostics.
[7] DSM-5. pp. 50–59.

features, but this does not necessarily mean that someone who is tested positively for these features would necessarily receive a diagnosis. *Autism*, or autism spectrum disorder, is by many clinicians still considered a clinical disorder after all, based on an estimate of what is best for a person with a certain request for help.

For many people however—researchers, clinicians and autistic people themselves—autism refers to a specific neurological and biological reality. The term 'neurodiversity', for instance, which is often used by advocates for the rights of autistic people, explicitly refers to a neurological difference. This is why autism, as a characteristic of someone's biology, should be conceived of as a difference and an identity—like homosexuality—rather than as a disease that we must cure. Society should invest in support and acceptance, rather than in the quest for a medicine or therapy for the 'redemption' of autism.[8] Interestingly so, the arguments based on a belief in the biological foundations of autism are also being used by researchers who plead for further research on genetics and neurology of autism, since the findings of such a study would help to develop a biologically founded therapy.[9]

The idea that autism is a condition that is caused by a specific genetic makeup has gained in popularity the past decades. This is certainly partly due to the fact that, under the influence of psychoanalyst Bruno Bettelheim,[10] for a long time people thought that autism was caused by distant behaviour of the mother during the first years of the child's life.[11] The theory was that, as a response to—and a defence against—this parental rejection, the child withdrew in itself. Ideas such as these cause huge feelings of guilt in—particularly—these mothers. The search for a biological cause of autism, such as a genetic cause, can also be regarded in this light: for parents—and mostly mothers—who were accused of contributing to the autism of their children, the notion that autism could be a genetic condition—which cannot be prevented—came as a relief.

Traditionally, a difference is made between *syndromal* and *idiopathic* autism. In the first case, autism is an expression of an underlying (genetic) syndrome, such as Fragile-X. In this case, the biological cause is known. In the second case, the biological cause of autism is not (yet) known, but it is

---

[8] Jaarsma and Welin (2012).
[9] Hens, Peeters and Dierickx (2016).
[10] Bettelheim (1972).
[11] Nadesan (2005).

generally presumed that there is one. As our knowledge about genetics and neurology is increasing, it is possible that the difference between these two is becoming less relevant. We still have to wait to see whether a definite genetic cause can be found in all cases of autism. There is an increasing amount of proof that genetic variations associated with autism are common variants, which means that they can also be found in the neurotypical population (i.e. people without an autism diagnosis).[12] Moreover, there is growing evidence that autism could be caused by an interaction between genetic and environmental factors. It has been known for a long time that autism is more frequent in children who are born prematurely. The ingestion of fine particles during pregnancy or the father's age at the time of conception also seems to have an effect. In her book *Rethinking Autism*, Lynn Waterhouse comes with an abundance of results from genetic studies and brain research, after which she concludes that it is probably not a good strategy to consider autism as a disorder that originates from a certain biological reality. It is after all very unlikely that such a reality is found: it is better to consider autism to be two behavioural symptoms, which can be the result of a big variety of genetic or neurological conditions, just as fever is a symptom of an underlying condition.[13]

However, the fact that autism is related to one or more neurological or cognitive realities which are different from typical neurological or cognitive functioning cannot be denied. Still, it is currently unclear whether a uniform neurological/cognitive explanation can be found at all for this different functioning. Perhaps there really are various (or innumerable) autisms. There are, for instance, various cognitive–psychological theories that try to explain autistic behaviour. The most renowned is the one that claims that autistic people supposedly have a deficient Theory of Mind (ToM). In philosophy and psychology, ToM refers to the ability to explain and predict the behaviour of others by attributing it to mental states such as beliefs, desires, intentions and emotions. Autistic people, for instance, are considered to find it difficult to imagine that others have intentions, too. As a consequence, they are also considered to have little insight into their own experiences.[14] It should be noted here, however, that a lack of ToM can also be related to other conditions and that autistic people do—albeit in some cases a bit later—develop a ToM. Whether a lack of ToM in

---

[12] Hens, Peeters and Dierickx (2016).
[13] Waterhouse (2013, pp. 432–436).
[14] Frith and Happé (1999), Baron-Cohen, Leslie and Frith (1985).

others automatically implies a lack of Theory of Own Mind—the awareness of an own self—is also still not clarified.

Other theories state that the primary deficit with autism is related to a *weak central coherence*.[15] Autistic people for instance supposedly get lost in details and have problems to connect the different details in order to create a unity. A variation on this hypothesis is that autistic people supposedly have a version of *context blindness*.[16] This would mean that they have more problems extracting extra information from the context. According to a third theory, autistic people supposedly have *weak executive functions*. As a consequence, autistic people supposedly have problems planning and organising things, and find it difficult to simultaneously coordinate different activities. This makes it difficult to take the next step, for instance in an argumentation, which could partly be the reason why they often have trouble with change.

Several more recent theories localise autism in differences on a basic level, for instance sensory perception or motor skills. An example hereof is the *Intense World Theory*, which localises the origin of autistic behaviour in neurobiology: local neural microcircuits supposedly hyperfunction, which makes people unable to sensibly process sensory input.[17] This theory is popular with many autists, because it fits very well with what they experience themselves. In the DSM-5, differences in sensory perception have for the first time been included as one of the possible manifestations of 'restrictive and repetitive behaviours'. In her book *Autism: A Social and Medical History*, Mitzi Waltz has the following to say about this:

> In the DSM-5, for the first time sensory-perceptual issues will appear as something that may affect people with autism and might be considered when making a diagnosis, though not yet as a diagnostic criterion. It is remarkable that it has taken so long for the internal experience of autism, rather than aspects of autism that may puzzle or bother non-autistic people, to become part of how it is officially defined.[18]

A more recent theory, *High, Inflexible Precision of Prediction Errors in Autism* (HIPPEA), has been developed by Sander van de Cruys and colleagues. He argues that autism might have to do with a lacking predictive

---
[15] Frith (2003).
[16] Vermeulen (2009).
[17] Markram, Rinaldi, Markram (2007).
[18] Waltz (2013, p. vi).

coding. Autistic people supposedly have problems with—based on the context—predicting the uncertainty of incoming information. Because of this, they would sometimes draw the wrong conclusions from information that is very context-sensitive. With respect to information where the context has a negative influence on accurate perception, such as optical illusion, they make less mistakes. They regard everything as 'new' information, and therefore prefer circumstances that are predictable.[19]

Still, many questions remain open. Is weak central coherence for instance the cause of all the other problems, such as executive functions? Are all these deficits the consequence of other, underlying causes at the level of information processing? Or are there various kinds of autism, which may appear to be similar behaviourally, but in fact one theory is based on overzealous neurons and the other on a deficit in ToM? In *The Philosophy of Autism*, Nick Pentzell, who has a diagnosis of autism himself, describes how "sensory overload inhibits *anyone* from thinking about much more than surviving its barrage."[20] That children with autism often score less on tests that are focused on assessing the understanding of intentions or thoughts of others, could be because of the fact that during the test, they already suffer from the amount of stimuli to such an extent that they can no longer sensibly participate in the test. Or that these children, because they suffer from sensory overstimulation at a very young age, develop a ToM considerably later than neurotypical children. The opinion people have about what autism really 'is' also has consequences for the question how one should ethically deal with autistic people. If the theories that take a different way of sensory processing—or information processing—as a starting point are correct, should therapy then not first and foremost be focused on relieving the pressure this involves, and not on teaching or training a ToM? And if it is true that behind the symptom autism, several possible explanations and several primordial deficits can be found, we think it would be extremely important to start looking even more individually at which approach is of importance to which individual.

We think there are at least three layers of meaning that concern the concept of autism and that—contrary to the biology of autism—are not yet examined extensively enough. The first layer is *the popular meaning of autism*. Although autism professionals emphasise that every individual

---

[19] Van de Cruys et al. (2014).
[20] Pentzell (2013).

with a diagnosis is different, autism as a concept does have certain connotations that are difficult to ignore. In the book *Representing Autism. Culture, Narrative, Fascination*, Stuart Murray describes how autism is depicted in books, films and other art forms: as neurological difference or uniqueness, and as a disease that should be overcome.[21] The way in which autism is depicted has several important implications. Erving Goffman and others have demonstrated that when you are told that you have a certain characteristic or identity X, this influences your self-image.[22] Philosopher of science Ian Hacking calls this *the looping effect*: classification changes that which or whom is being classified and vice versa.[23] People can identify with categories, but also reject and transform them.

Apart from the popular meaning of autism, it can also be seen as a *cultural phenomenon*, which we will call the second layer. Again, we could look at this from several perspectives. It could be possible that the fact that we consider autism in itself to be a singular phenomenon is exactly the result of the fact that we only have one name for the different underlying disorders or differences. Moreover, what autism means and whether it means something depends on the time and place. The historical evolution of the concept has already been described by several authors, including the Dutch psychiatrist Berend Verhoeff. He describes how, throughout history, the term 'autism' has referred to different things.[24] Verhoeff argues that the children whom Leo Kanner described mid-twentieth century, possibly did not have the same disorders as the people we now call autistic. He argues that the idea that the diagnostic criteria have broadened is not entirely true: the meaning of autism has shifted a few times throughout the history of autism, which resulted in the fact that it is not clear at all what—throughout history—exactly is referred to when people speak about autism. This is why, says Verhoeff, we should not assume that we can find one and the same biological reality under the concept of 'autism'. Gil Eyal and his colleagues of Columbia University in New York argue in their book *The Autism Matrix* that the current increase in diagnoses of autism is due to diagnostic substitution of 'mental retardation' by 'autism spectrum disorder', and also due to the fact that children with mental disorders were—in the mid-1900s—deinstitutionalized. Since this meant

[21] Murray (2008).
[22] Goffman (1963).
[23] Hacking (1996).
[24] Verhoeff (2013a, b, 2015).

that the child was cared for at home, it was up to the parents to start looking for adequate help. What also contributed to the increase in diagnoses of autism was that a range of services and therapies that were not available for ('plain') intellectual disability, *were* available for the support of autism. A final, but certainly not unimportant contributor to this trend has to do with imaging. Intellectual disability used to have the connotation of being something insurmountable.[25] It is important to keep in mind that autism can at the same time—throughout various cultures—refer to different things, and that a certain neurological characteristic which we would call autistic in one culture, would possibly not stand out at all—or does not even have to be designated—in another culture. After all, the extent to which we consider something to be a *disorder* is closely connected to what we consider to be normal behaviour.[26] On the one hand there are, for instance, cultures where it is not expected at all—or where it is even considered to be inappropriate—that children make contact with adults or when they spontaneously mingle in conversations of adults. On the other hand, our western culture, with its abundance of stimuli and penchant for quick chats, may consider or perceive certain neurological differences as pathological sooner than in a different era or environment.

The third layer of meaning is about what it means for the diagnosed person to have a diagnosis of autism. Because, even though more attention has been given recently to values and opinions of people with a diagnosis of autism—for instance, when dealing with the goals of scientific research—[27]considerably less research has been done on what such a diagnosis means for the individual itself. Although, in recent years such research has taken a giant step forward.[28] For example, autistic scholars have been publishing books about their own experiences and that of other autistic adults,[29] and the book *Aquamarine Blue 5* describes the educational experience of autists in college and at university.[30] Moreover, there is a growing number of initiatives in different countries that ensure the participation of autists in research priority settings, such as the PARC initiative in the UK

---

[25] Eyal (2010, p. 33).
[26] Kim (2012).
[27] Fletcher-Watson et al. (2017), Nicolaidis et al. (2015), Yusuf and Elsabbagh (2015), Pellicano, Dinsmore and Charman (2014), Pellicano and Stears (2011).
[28] Huws and Jones (2008).
[29] Milton (2017), Beardon (2017).
[30] Prince-Hughes (2002).

(Participatory Autism Research Collective) and LAVA, an initiative in Belgium by autistic people that provides input and advice to Belgian researchers.

Relatively little research has been done querying autistic people in Flanders and the Netherlands about their experience with autism and with the diagnosis. In this book, we started from the assumption that research on the experiences and perceptions of people with a diagnosis of autism can be valuable to come to a better understanding of how a diagnosis works and what it means to feel different. We have interviewed 22 adults who have been diagnosed with autism, autism spectrum disorder or Asperger at some point in their lives.

Methodology

As a guideline for setting up the interviews, we have used a phenomenological method. We do think that the phenomenological dimension of autism is essential in order to better understand the ethical and philosophical implications of 'having autism', and that this is at least as important as bio-causal explanatory models. As Wouter Kusters states in his book *De filosofie van de waanzin*:

> (…) when you start reducing *something* -– whether it is mind, love or madness, and whether the result is called matter, hormones or neurons – you will always first have to know *what* it is you reduce.[31]

Given the several layers of meaning of the concept of autism, we believe that a phenomenological approach is very appropriate to help us understand, not so much what autism might be biologically, but rather what autism *means*.

The use of a phenomenological interview method means that we set our own presumptions about autism aside, and assume that the lived reality of having a diagnosis of autism is an important source of information.[32] In the set-up of our interviews, and while discussing our results, we used the method of the Interpretative Phenomenological Analysis (IPA), a qualitative research method which is specifically appropriate to study experiences

---

[31] Kusters (2014, p. 28).
[32] Van Manen (1990, 2014).

of respondents in the context of life events.[33] IPA is characterised by a double hermeneutics: the interpretation of the respondents' own experiences by the respondents themselves and our analysis of these experiences and interpretations. IPA is also a method that focuses on the idiographic, rather than trying to generalise experiences. This is why we always outline the context of the respondents' statements and then assess how these experiences fit within that context. We do indeed assume that this reality is understandable, and that the experiences our interviewees describe are not entirely different from other human experiences and realities. We also assume that our participants can recount their own experiences in a credible way, just as credible as if they were not in possession of a diagnosis. The stance that self-reflections of autistic people are not credible because of their deficient ToM is not something we endorse. We will further explore this in Chap. 6: *The (In)ability to Self-Reflect*.

In the spring of 2016, we started to recruit respondents by publishing an announcement of the study on the website of the Vlaamse Vereniging Autisme (*Flemish Autism Association, VVA*) and on social media such as Facebook and Twitter. Two participants are acquaintances of Raymond or Kristien. The condition for participation was that people had to be at least 18 years old, and that they had to have a diagnosis of autism, autism spectrum disorder or syndrome of Asperger. An overview of the participants can be found in Table 1.1. Because of methodological restrictions, we only examined the experiences of individuals who were aware of their diagnosis. It should be noted that our study was conducted in 2016, which means that all data in the schedule below—as well as any references made in the interviews—refers to the situation in 2016.

One limitation of our study could be that we were not able to examine the experiences of people who are not aware that they have a diagnosis of autism. Because our research question also concerns the experience of having a diagnosis, we are of the opinion that this limitation is not of significant importance. On top of that, we are not looking to generalise conceptions of autism, but rather to describe a wide variety of experiences. We also purposely did not ask the participants to show us their diagnostic report or tell us their IQ, since we did not want to let this influence our perception or interpretation. Moreover, we wanted to let the participants decide, on their own initiative, whether they thought it was important to inform us about the contents of the report. Here, our study clearly differs

[33] Smith (2009).

Table 1.1 Overview of participants

Chosen name	Age	Gender	Interview type
Carl	55	M	Oral
Bluetopian	47	M	Chat
Baukis	60	F	Oral
Sandra	38	F	Oral
Robyn	30	F	Oral
Sofie	53	F	Oral
Marie	41	F	Chat
Michael	26	M	Oral
ASSpirin[a]	53	F	Chat
Albert	46	M	Email
Hannah	36	F	Oral
Samuel	43	M	Chat
Tatiana	51	F	Oral
Nora	28	F	Oral
Matteo	36	M	Oral
Bas	35	M	Oral
Els	47	F	Oral
Vic	39	M	Oral
BartDelam	46	M	Oral
Kris	46	M	Oral
Mickey	27	M	Oral

[a] This respondent chose the name "ASSpirientje", which refers to (1) the Dutch word for Aspirin (*aspirine*) and (2) the Dutch abbreviation for ASD (ASS, *Autisme Spectrum Stoornis*). For the purposes of the English translation, we therefore chose the name "ASSpirin"

from the more traditional autism studies, where people do wish to make a distinction based on IQ or other measured characteristics.

Another limitation to our study could be that people who applied may have a tendency to experience their diagnosis as positive. It is possible that those who resist their diagnosis, or those who did not choose to turn to psychiatric diagnostics themselves, are less tempted to participate in such a study. And indeed, the majority of our interviewees appeared to have a very positive attitude towards the fact that they were diagnosed. It would therefore be good to repeat this study with participants who, for instance, have always known that they have a diagnosis of autism. Also, the majority of people we interviewed had only recently received their diagnosis. This may affect how they experience their diagnosis, but it also gave us the opportunity to explore the experiences of people who were still actively in the process of coming to terms with the diagnosis. It would be very interesting to do further research on experiences of being diagnosed over an extended period of time: immediately after the diagnosis, five years after, ten years after… and then compare those experiences and see how perspectives may or may not shift.

Given the fact that some people with a diagnosis of autism are not quite comfortable with an oral interview, we offered the applicants the choice between an oral interview, a chat session or an email conversation. They were also free to choose the location where the interview took place. Some people told us that they wanted to see the interview guide beforehand, which we allowed. After each conversation, we told the participants that they—should they wish to add things to their story—were always free to contact us via email or other media. One participant afterwards decided to withdraw from the project.

The questions we used during the interview can be found in Table 1.2. We chose to not immediately start with the subject of diagnostics and autism, but to first allow the people to tell us something about themselves: what they enjoy, what their anxieties are… With many participants, the subject autism was addressed spontaneously although they were aware that autism was a major topic of the project in general. We did not strictly follow the order of the questions as shown in Table 1.2. We also used an open-ended interview style wherein we tried to focus intently on certain aspects that were important to the participants.

The oral interviews were transcribed afterwards. Since the participants spoke or wrote about their personal experiences, the transcripts or chat sessions may contain sensitive information. Prior to the interview, we provided the participants with an information sheet which explained that the interview material would be coded, and that in the final publication, we would use a name they could choose themselves, for instance a pseudonym. Participants have signed an informed letter of consent. The conversation material is secured with a password. The study protocol, the information sheet and the letter of consent have been approved by the *Ethische Adviescommissie Sociale en Humane Wetenschappen* (Ethical Advisory Committee Social Sciences and Humanities) of the University of Antwerp.

All interviews took place between June 2016 and August 2016, and were immediately transcribed (Kristien Hens 12 and Raymond Langenberg 10 interviews). The analysis was performed inductively: we did not use a theoretical framework when we first looked at the data. We individually

Table 1.2 Interview schedule

Who are you?
Please tell us something about yourself. How would you describe yourself?
  Which things do you like? What did you used to like (as a child, as a young adult)
  What activities do you enjoy? (Why do you enjoy this? What do you experience when doing this? How would you interpret this yourself? What do you think about that? What do these enjoyable moments mean to you?)
  What do you worry about? Why do you think you worry about exactly that?
  What are things that really bother you? If so, can you please tell us what they are? Can you explain to us what it means to you when you are really bothered by something?
  Please give an example of a situation that is *typical* to who you are. (Typical to what you experience, what you think, what you see, what you notice, how you react).
  Please tell us about a difficult situation you were involved in.
    Who were involved in it?
    What role did you have?
    How did you deal with it?
    What solutions did you find, or—when they did not come from you—what were the solutions?
  Which people are important to you? (Now, in the future, in the past). Can you explain what it means to you that something is 'important'? With whom do you enjoy getting in contact?

Being different
Do you have the feeling that you are different than others?
  What does being different than others mean to you?
  What is deviant to you?
  Wherein do you consider yourself to be the same as others?
  Is it important to be the same? Can you demonstrate this with an example or anecdote?
Do you sometimes have the idea that others exhibit deviant behaviour?
How did you discover that?
  Did it come from you or from others?
  Wherein lies that being different? How you deal with the 'other'? How you see or interpret things? How you hear and feel? Is there an event that comes to mind that can help you explain this?
When did you first discover that you regard, experience and perceive things differently than others?
Which experiences have caused you to discover that there were differences between you and the others?
  How did you deal with these experiences? Can you also give examples of that?
  Which events have led to your diagnosis?
  What does it mean to you to experience that difference?

(*continued*)

Table 1.2 (continued)

Diagnosis
How did you come to the conclusion to start a diagnosis procedure?
What did you think about the diagnostic process?
  Did you have doubts?
  Who questioned you?
  How were you questioned?
  How was that for you?
  Which tests did you do, what did you think about the tests?
What do you now, afterwards, think about the whole process?
  Did it help you?
  Does it make you think differently about yourself?
  Did it teach you new things about yourself which you did not know before?
What did that diagnosis mean to you when it was just made? What does the diagnosis mean now?
How do you involve the diagnosis in thinking about yourself?
Closing Question
Is there something you wish to add? Is there a question you would like to ask yourself?

wrote down themes in the margins of the printed transcripts. In the period from September 2016 to December 2016, we had biweekly meetings where we discussed our notes, analysed the documented experiences and merged the themes we had a consensus over into larger categories. In that stage, relevant quotations were already selected. These categories are represented in the chapter headings of this book, which were organically ranked in a logical thematic structure afterwards. Based on the interviews, we discovered a kind of logic, a common thread running through all the stories of the interviewees. In the different stories, similar courses become visible, displayed in consecutive chapters. After a first draft of the texts, we asked the participants to give feedback on the interpretation of the respective quotes. All participants have provided suggestions to improve the quotes and our interpretation of them. We have incorporated all these suggestions, except for one respondent, who withdrew from the project afterwards.

The following chapters successively describe experiences of being different; experiences of suffering that have motivated people to seek help; experiences with the tests as such; the interpretation people have given to their diagnosis as being an explanation for their uniqueness on the one hand, but on the other hand also as a challenge of having to relate to the stereotypes that are connected to the concept of autism, and with which they may not identify. The book ends with an elaboration on how the participants come to self-reflection, which means of expression they use for that and also how our participants think about care. Each chapter is preceded by a drawing by Raymond Langenberg. Indeed, as the autistic experience often implies having different preferences for communication, besides purely oral communication, we believe that these drawings, which reflect Raymond's own reaction to the interview, should be considered as an equally important source of information as the written text.

BIBLIOGRAPHY

Baron-Cohen, S., A.M. Leslie, and U. Frith. 1985. Does the Autistic Child Have a 'Theory of Mind. *Cognition* 21 (1): 37–46. Elsevier, October.

Beardon, Luke. 2017. *Autism and Asperger Syndrome in Adults*. London: Sheldon Press.

Bettelheim, Bruno. 1972. *The Empty Fortress: Infantile Autism and the Birth of the Self*. New edition edition. S.l. New York: Free Press.

Beyers, Leo. 2014. *Het wordende denken*. Antwerp: Maklu.

Eyal, Gil, ed. 2010. *The Autism Matrix: The Social Origins of the Autism Epidemic*. Cambridge/Malden, MA: Polity.

Fletcher-Watson, Sue, Fabio Apicella, Bonnie Auyeung, Stepanka Beranova, Frederique Bonnet-Brilhault, Ricardo Canal-Bedia, Tony Charman, et al. 2017. Attitudes of the Autism Community to Early Autism Research. *Autism* 21 (1): 61–74. Sage journals.

Frith, Uta. 2003. *Autism: Explaining the Enigma*. 2nd ed. Malden: Blackwell Pub.

Frith, U., and F. Happé. 1999. Theory of Mind and Self-Consciousness: What Is It Like to Be Autistic? *Mind and Language* 14 (1): 1–22. Wiley.

Goffman, Erving. 1963. *Stigma. Notes on the Management of Spoiled Identity*. Englewood Cliffs: Prentice Hall.

Hacking, Ian. 1996. The Looping Effects of Human Kinds. In *Causal Cognition*, ed. Dan Sperber, David Premack, and Ann James Premack, 351–383. New York: Oxford University Press.

Hens, Kristien, Hilde Peeters, and Kris Dierickx. 2016. The Ethics of Complexity. Genetics and Autism, a Literature Review. *American Journal of Medical Genetics Part B: Neuropsychiatric Genetics 171(B)* (3): 305–316. Wiley-Blackwell.

Huws, J.C., and R.S.P. Jones. 2008. Diagnosis, Disclosure, and Having Autism: An Interpretative Phenomenological Analysis of the Perceptions of Young People with Autism. *Journal of Intellectual & Developmental Disability* 33 (2): 99–107. Informa.

Jaarsma, Pier, and Stellan Welin. 2012. Autism as a Natural Human Variation: Reflections on the Claims of the Neurodiversity Movement. *Health Care Analysis* 20 (1): 20–30. Springer.

Kanner, Leo. 1968. Autistic Disturbances of Affective Contact. *Acta Paedopsychiatrica* 35 (4): 100–136. Schwabe.
Kim, Hyun Uk. 2012. Autism Across Cultures: Rethinking Autism. *Disability & Society* 27 (4): 535–545. Taylor & Francis, June 1.
Kusters, Wouter. 2014. *Filosofie van de Waanzin*. Rotterdam: Lemniscaat.
Markram, H., Tania Rinaldi, and Kamila Markram. 2007. The Intense World Syndrome – An Alternative Hypothesis for Autism. *Frontiers in Neuroscience* 1 (1): 77–96. Frontiers media, October 15.
Milton, Damian. 2017. *A Mismatch of Salience*. Hove: Pavilion Publishing.
Murray, Stuart. 2008. *Representing Autism: Culture, Narrative, Fascination*. Liverpool: Liverpool University Press.
Nadesan, Majia Holmer. 2005. *Constructing Autism: Unravelling the "Truth" and Understanding the Social*. London/New York: Routledge.
Nicolaidis, Christina, Dora M. Raymaker, Elesia Ashkenazy, Katherine E. McDonald, Sebastian Dern, Amelia E.V. Baggs, Steven K. Kapp, Michael Weiner, and W. Cody Boisclair. 2015. 'Respect the Way I Need to Communicate with You': Healthcare Experiences of Adults on the Autism Spectrum. *Autism* 19 (7): 824–831. Sage Journals, October 1.
Pellicano, Elizabeth, and Marc Stears. 2011. Bridging Autism, Science and Society: Moving Toward an Ethically Informed Approach to Autism Research. *Autism Research: Official Journal of the International Society for Autism Research* 4 (4): 271–282. INSAR, August.
Pellicano, Elizabeth, Adam Dinsmore, and Tony Charman. 2014. What Should Autism Research Focus Upon? Community Views and Priorities from the United Kingdom. *Autism* 18 (7): 756–770. Sage Journals, October.
Pentzell, Nick. 2013. I Think, Therefore I Am. I Am Verbal, Therefore I Live. In *The Philosophy of Autism*, ed. Jami L. Anderson and Simon Cushing, 103–108. Lanham: Rowman & Littlefield.
Prince-Hughes, Dawn. 2002. *Aquamarine Blue 5*. Athens: Swallow Press.
Smith, Jonathan. 2009. *Interpretative Phenomenological Analysis: Theory, Method and Research*. 1st ed. Los Angeles: Sage.
Van de Cruys, Kris Evers Sander, Ruth Van der Hallen, Lien Van Eylen, Bart Boets, Lee de-Wit, and Johan Wagemans. 2014. Precise Minds in Uncertain Worlds: Predictive Coding in Autism. *Psychological Review* 121 (4): 649–675. American Psychological Association, October.
Van Manen, Max. 1990. *Researching Lived Experience: Human Science for an Action Sensitive Pedagogy*. 2nd ed. Albany: State University of New York Press.
———. 2014. *Phenomenology of Practice: Meaning-Giving Methods in Phenomenological Research and Writing*. Walnut Creek: Routledge.
Verhoeff, Berend. 2013a. Autism in Flux: A History of the Concept from Leo Kanner to DSM-5. *History of Psychiatry* 24 (4): 442–458. Sage Publications, December 1.

———. 2013b. The Autism Puzzle: Challenging a Mechanistic Model on Conceptual and Historical Grounds. *Philosophy, Ethics, and Humanities in Medicine 8* (1): 17. Springer.

———. 2015. Fundamental Challenges for Autism Research: The Science-Practice Gap, Demarcating Autism and the Unsuccessful Search for the Neurobiological Basis of Autism. *Medicine, Health Care, and Philosophy* 18 (3): 443–447. Springer, August.

Vermeulen, Peter. 2009. *Autisme Als Contextblindheid*. Leuven: Acco.

Waltz, Mitzi. 2013. *Autism. A Social and Medical History*. Hampshire: Palgrave Macmillan.

Waterhouse, Lynn. 2013. *Rethinking Autism: Variation and Complexity*. London/Waltham, MA: Academic.

Yusuf, Afiqah, and Mayada Elsabbagh. 2015. At the Cross-Roads of Participatory Research and Biomarker Discovery in Autism: The Need for Empirical Data. *BMC Medical Ethics* 16: 88.

CHAPTER 2

Being 'Different'

Abstract This chapter explores the experiences of our interviewees with respect to their own being 'different'. How did they notice they were not the same as others? How do they think they deviate from the norm? And what do they think and how do they feel about that? This chapter provides us with numerous stories from people who have had first-hand experience of not fitting in that share the strange situations they found themselves in.

Keywords Autism • Difference • Experience • Challenges

Many of the stories our respondents tell display a similar historical pattern. A great number of them explain that they felt different than the other children when they were young, and this initial experience has for many of them been the motivation for deeper research into their own 'being different'. In books and academic articles, people often speak of the *enigma* called autism, that is, the renowned work of autism researcher Uta Frith, *Autism. Explaining the Enigma*.[1] Frith claims that our autistic fellow

[1] Frith (2003).

human beings are qualitatively different from the average person, both socially and with respect to certain interests. Using this kind of symbolism, the person with a diagnosis is portrayed as difficult to read, as a puzzle to be solved.

Even though there is a lot of thorough knowledge available about the phenomenon of 'being different' with respect to autism, mostly from the viewpoint of medical professionals or caregivers, we have chosen to let our interviewees bare witness to how they experience their own 'being different'. Some of them have always had the feeling that they functioned differently, that they notice different aspects of an event and that they are sometimes more bothered by what happens than others. Other interviewees only sensed this being different when they reached adulthood. Many of them, however, explain that they were able to understand experiences or behaviours from the past better after the diagnosis.

Needless to say, we will face a few obstacles when we ask questions regarding people's being or feeling different. Every person is more or less unique and different, so what are we talking about when we address the theme of 'being different'? Do we perhaps need the inevitable other to tell us? When discussing topics of this nature, we easily enter an area of ambiguities, experiences and perceptions. This is, however, the area par excellence where people with a diagnosis of autism seem to show a large number of similarities. In this chapter, our participants start by describing what 'feeling different' means to them. After that, we will elaborate on specific experiences of time, space and events, which all lead to the conclusion that people with a diagnosis indeed respond, think and feel differently than others.

The quotations below show that the interviewees make their own report of their experiences and perceptions. They are, however, also faced with the impossibility to determine what exactly is different about the experience that others—who they perceive to be normal—have. A multitude of coincidental events can cause someone to conclude that he or she reacts differently or is less flexible. Carl (55), diagnosed with Asperger's syndrome at 42, explains:

> *So my internal 'knowing', shall I say, is like: I must do something with that, I must make sure that I learn to think, I must make sure that I deal with that. How do you call it, is that a conscience or something, or your self-reflection? But on the other hand, to the outside world, I have an enormous need to conceal that there is something wrong with me or that there is something different. You see? So you actually try to remain as inconspicuous as possible, to avoid being faced*

with that being different by the outside world. And yes, being called to account for this and yes, I don't know if that's different than others. But deep down, you know: I'm going to have to do something about this someday. [Carl]

Respondents refer to a continuous stream of experiences in daily life that illustrates their previously mentioned 'responding differently'. Via daily experiences—along with some extreme experiences—they start to reflect on the difference between themselves and others around them. Self-knowledge—which often first presents itself in early childhood—only very gradually evolves into the awareness that this difference means being truly different. Still, it is often not easy to phrase or completely know this difference. It can consist of experiencing small daily misunderstandings: becoming aware of the fact that you assess things differently than others, noticing that you apparently see different things than many others, perceiving that you have understood agreements differently than the other... It is a succession of little mistakes as it were, which others seem to be able to get over easily. The person who experiences those mistakes finds this much more difficult however. And thus, a concern arises: if that one thing is understood incorrectly, what about all the other moments of attunement? Our respondents often mention how they have less tolerance for sound, brightness or smell than others. These others sometimes appear to be more flexible and less out of balance in the same and similar situations. These kinds of experiences, and the observation that this is a daily reality, can eventually lead to the conclusion that one may indeed be different than everyone else.

Bluetopian (47), diagnosed with an autism spectrum disorder (ASD) and non-verbal learning disorder (NLD) a few months before the interview, compares it with a fast luxury car that looks like a BMW or a Mercedes, but only has a two-stroke engine inside and is therefore unable to perform as one would expect from a luxury car.

> *Yes. I have always thought, because I pay attention to details, that my work is precise. But the tests demonstrate that this is not the case. Especially when the pressure increases, I don't work detailed and precise. What a shock! Apparently, attention to detail has always been a coping strategy. Quite energy consuming... but I can't help it, because otherwise I'll blunder time after time... You see... again tempted to bring up the image of a Mercedes or BMW... while there is only the capacity of a two-stroke engine... I still don't have the concrete answer to: "What now?", and that is frustrating. It's mainly exhausting. It would be better if I let things go: handbrake off and we'll see...* [Bluetopian]

If nothing comes naturally, like it seems to come to others, insecurity and the fear that there is something wrong increase. For some respondents, it has taken years until they even dared to acknowledge to themselves that sometimes, they have different experiences or that they respond differently than others. It often takes time to be able to see that this being different is not just an ordinary difference of who one is, or that one simply experiences things in one's own way. The moment when it starts to sink in that—apart from the explicable and natural difference there is between all human beings—there is also something fundamentally different, is also not the same for everyone. Most of our respondents were only faced with this when a certain line was crossed, and it became too much for them to handle.

Some of the participants describe the feeling of being different as a general feeling of being 'from another planet', of not really belonging here. Tatiana (51), diagnosed with the syndrome of Asperger a few months before the interview, describes it as follows:

> *It's not easy for me to go outside. I don't experience this with all people, but I do for instance when I walk the streets. I see people go to work, while I have always felt a loner, even as if I'm from another planet.* [Tatiana]

Further on in the conversation, Tatiana points out that she likes having people around, but that the feeling of not fitting in causes her to prefer being alone. Robyn refers to autistic people as 'dogs in a world of cats'. Another participant, Mickey, says he feels that he is playing a part in *The Truman Show*. *The Truman Show* (1998) is a movie where the main character is unaware of the fact that his whole life is actually a world-famous reality show and that he is the protagonist. At a certain moment, a couple of anomalies and the help of a member of the public—who cannot bear to watch it anymore—make Truman realise what is really going on. Both the references to being 'from another planet' and *The Truman Show* are about the feeling of being the odd one out. In both cases, people feel that they have no access to certain information that is freely available to others. The others, the normal people, *do* seem to fit in this world. This feeling is also illustrated in the next quotation, where BartDelam (46)—diagnosed with autism spectrum disorder for four years—describes his feeling that people are laughing at him:

> *I take other people's remarks, which are intended to be funny, way too seriously. When someone makes a small mistake, people sometimes make well-intended*

> jokes such as "Wake up, sleepyhead", "You're not the sharpest tool in the box, are you?", "Forgot your glasses?"... These kinds of remarks are having an increasingly strong effect on me. I don't really think they're jokes and it seems I take them literally. Instead of laughing heartily with my own mistakes, I go into defence mode and try to explain what has gone wrong. Rationally, I know that these remarks should not be taken seriously and that others don't expect that I start defending myself. Now I just laugh, along with the others, although actually I still don't think it's funny. When I see other people laughing and I don't know what they're laughing about, I immediately think they're laughing at me. [BartDelam]

Some of the participants refer to periods before the diagnosis, and even to their childhood, in order to illustrate that this feeling of being different and not fitting in at all has always been there. Tatiana explains:

> I was very lonely as a child. I really wanted to have friends to do things with that I liked, but they always wanted to do different things. As a child, I would do very strange things, just to fit in. I think I can really just remember that I was always playing by myself in the sandbox, or that I would eat worms or something. [Tatiana]

As a result of not fitting in at all, Tatiana tried so hard that she started to do extreme things in order to fit in. What took the form of eating worms as a child to impress her peers, evolved into more extreme behaviour during her teens. Unfortunately, this behaviour did not have the effect she hoped for.

Some of the participants never realised they functioned differently until after the diagnostics. Robyn (30), diagnosed with autism a few months before the interview, reveals how her psychologist asked her why she said "sorry I'm too early" in a certain conversation:

> And that was for me one of the first times I went like: "Ah, you guys really think differently." Because I am thinking: how can I keep a conversation going, how does this person act and what should I say now, and am I saying it correctly. While you guys think about how that person is feeling. And that is something I don't think about at all, no, that was something for me... that was very strange to realise. [Robyn]

For Robyn, "sorry, I'm too early" just meant "hello", while she thinks that neurotypical people are more concerned about each other's feelings.

What actually *is* this being different? And in what respect is being different necessarily so bad? Bluetopian defines autism as a disorder, not necessarily because it is 'bad', but because it means you don't belong to the regular order. That is why it is—not necessarily for himself, but because he experiences that 'others' and society in general apparently expect this—important to be the same as the great majority:

I don't in any way agree that autism is a 'quality', a 'blessing'... It is definitely a disorder because it deviates from the ordinary. [Bluetopian]

The fact that being different (because of autism) is seen as a disorder because it implies that you deviate from what people consider to be normal, seems at first tautological. Still, this quote is very clarifying. Not conforming results in the fact that the other can become a threat. Samuel (43) describes it as follows:

Being different mostly means to me not understanding what others do, doing something completely different, that others think what I do is strange, and vice versa. It mostly means that others are threatening to me because they appear fickle and unpredictable. [Samuel]

Because you are different than the other, and you don't understand him or her because of it, the other can come across as threatening. Samuel also describes how 'being deviant' automatically implies that others want to correct or repair you:

Being deviant means that you perceive and give meaning to things differently, in the sense that it is a contribution to chaos and therefore must be removed. Most people want to remove the deviant in one way or another, either by imposing their own signification or by repairing it. [Samuel]

According to Samuel, being different means that you do not fit in the frame of reference of the ordinary fellow human being, and this is automatically a situation that must be corrected. As a 'different' person, you are a minority anyway and you miss out, as Bluetopian says:

Fundamentally, my biggest problem is: not being able to connect with others. Not really being able to connect with others. If YOU keep having problems to connect with OTHERS – where others are usually still able to find someone – you can hardly claim that the problem lies with all the others. YOU deviate. YOU are simply part of a minority. See the figures for prevalence of ASD in the general public. YOU deviate = I deviate. [Bluetopian]

According to Bluetopian, it is too often expected that the minority should conform to the majority, and it is an illusion to think that this majority will simply accept people being different. Sofie (52) has received the diagnosis of autism spectrum disorder two weeks prior to the interview. She describes how she experiences the feeling of being an outsider—now confirmed by a diagnosis—as an obstacle. She refers to her difficult childhood, which has always made her feel like an outsider.

As a child, I was never allowed to join youth clubs, I was only allowed to stay at home, between four walls. So I have always lived next to society. But now I want to live in society. I really pity myself when again I feel I'm on the outside. [Sofie]

Earlier on in the conversation, Sofie described that she often finds it difficult to keep a conversation going, to chat along at parties. She says it is important to be the same as everyone else in order to participate in society. She also really wants that. Achieving this remains difficult however.

Marie (41) was diagnosed with autism spectrum disorder a couple of months before the interview. Ever since she was a young child, Marie has had the feeling of not belonging in what she describes as a "strange world", which she generally experiences as complex and confusing. During the interview, she describes the trouble she has creating an overview from all the bits and pieces of information she observes in a defragmented state. She has often done her best to stand out as little as possible, to be quiet and remain in the background. Her own awareness of being different makes Marie's appreciation for others who are not entirely part of the group even greater:

Outsiders! Those who aren't – can't or don't want to be – part of a group, are or were bullied, who were probably all by themselves in the playground at school: I am drawn to them. Those who are 'different' than the masses, the outsiders, they don't fit in but don't want to stand out by desperately trying not to fit in either. [Marie]

Marie specifies it as follows:

Well, at school there were sometimes students who didn't want to fit in and dressed and behaved like punks or something, but with that behaviour, too, you could actually categorise them, and they were engaging with a majority, even if it was perhaps a small majority. The people I am talking about, are the people who didn't fit in and were excluded because others didn't consider them to be mainstream (enough). [Marie]

You cannot always do something about being different. It is not merely a matter of refusing to adapt. Some participants in our study expressed the feeling that the others are the ones that actually refuse to adapt. Bas (35), diagnosed a year before the interview, explains:

It is quite ironic, if people say: "autists stay within their cocoon", when it is actually the other way around. We have to transcend this cocoon every day, by understanding others who happen to be a majority, while it hardly ever happens the other way around. Who then, is staying in his cocoon? [Bas]

Bas and also some other respondents argue that life would be easier if everyone was autistic. Bas says that a cure for autism is an interesting thought-experiment, but that he actually does not want it. The outsider must transcend himself continuously, by participating in a world where the majority thinks differently, and the majority makes a lot less (to no) effort to empathise with the lifeworld of he who deviates from the norm in certain areas. In this context, Marie says: "Maybe we should put those pins on the market: 'I'm an autist, get used to it!'", but later she nuances:

My partner is also autistic and she is more bothered by loud music in a restaurant or supermarket than me. So I don't think that the majority who likes that music must do without it just because we can't stand it. I'm more like: ok let me get my earplugs. [Marie]

Matteo (36) received his diagnosis of autism nine years before the interview. He never really thought he was different from others, but he thinks this is maybe because he did not speak with others very often. He never noticed that he spoke very slowly until he heard a recording of himself. According to Matteo, the others were the ones who thought he was different. This caused some problems for him, for instance in job interviews. He enthusiastically responded to a job opening his job coach proposed to him, but he was not aware of how he came across. He only realised that after receiving feedback.

> *Yes that man from the recruitment agency had encouraged me, but that woman had said: "He speaks so slowly". And yes, that was apparently unpleasant for that woman, or that didn't come across well, but I wasn't aware of that during the conversation.* [Matteo]

Autism is often described as *processing information differently*. In various interviews, it became clear that people feel that their own thought processes are too slow. BartDelam explains:

> *What's typically me is that I'm actually never spontaneous and that I can't deal with unexpected issues. It's as if all stimuli first must pass through my brain and must be processed there. Everything has to be reasoned first. Because of this, my reactions can be delayed for a few seconds to a couple of minutes, but are almost never spontaneous and uncontrolled. I also very often worry about the same thing for hours, months even.* [BartDelam]

Still, this 'slowness' can also imply a certain 'thoroughness'. Some of our participants describe themselves as very eager to learn. They enjoy reading books, they like to learn new things and they have an eye for beauty.

In the quotation below, Albert (46)—diagnosed at 45 years—describes how he thinks things through much more thoroughly than others during meetings:

> *Before I say something, for instance at a meeting, I really think about all possible approaches and answers. This goes very far, covering all possible details, to the point of absurdity. After much deliberation, I come to an answer. I will only raise this when I am a 100% certain. This is why often, I don't have much to say. This does however make me notice things that others didn't think about.* [Albert]

This focus on thoroughness and details can cause people to get stuck. People get entangled in details and lose their overview. Tatiana uses a well-known metaphor of maps, with motorways and detours to describe how her mind works:

> *They all think I am very focused on detail and precise. There is an image with maps, roadmaps: most people are on the main roads and go from a to b via these main roads. But with me, those little brain paths have not died, so I am on the little country roads. I also remember them all, and then I'm not in fifth gear but I only drive in first gear. Or I walk. I think that's very typically me and*

I also think that's a good way to explain it. And I feel everything and I see everything and it's very heavy, very intense. It takes very long to sink in, but when it sinks in it's much heavier. [Tatiana]

Tatiana only slowly becomes aware of certain experiences, but once she feels them, they are intense. She gives the example of a telephone call she received from Sardinia when she was in a restaurant. Her adult daughter had been in a car accident. The person on the phone told Tatiana her daughter survived, which Tatiana experienced as a relief, after which she finished her meal. Only when she got home did she realise the severity of the situation. She called back and felt heavy emotions.

ASSpirin (53) was diagnosed with autism in December 2015. The quotation below is an excerpt of a chat session with us, in which she describes herself as "four ears and half a mouth". With this, she illustrates how she prefers to absorb many things first, before speaking herself. This makes her a person who listens well and feels intuitively what her conversation partner actually wants to say:

ASSpirin: *Four ears and half a mouth.*
ASSpirin: *That means that I see, feel and hear a lot which in individual conversations makes me come across as someone who listens very well.*
KH: *You have the idea that you hear everything much better or that you hear much more, do I understand this correctly?*
ASSpirin: *Not just hear, but also the body language and what's not being said.*

Sandra (38) who was 35 at the time of her diagnosis, also describes this attentiveness towards others:

They also very often say for instance that autists have no empathy. But I think that I have a lot more empathy than anyone, anyway than other people sometimes, just because I think that I am someone who observes everything. I observe everything, I look at everything, I think... I talk smoothly but I think about it and I know what I say. There is not a word of what I say that I don't agree with. But that is because I think a lot... It is not that I prepare every answer, it comes from within. [Sandra]

Sandra does not acknowledge this 'lack of empathy' that is sometimes associated with autism. She *has* empathy according to her own norms, and she senses a lot of things about people. Her problem is that she is not able to pinpoint it all spontaneously. By observing and thinking, she tries to assess if what she senses is correct in order to be able to respond appropriately.

Robyn does identify with the image of the autist who is unable to empathise with the other. She makes an explicit distinction between empathy and sympathy:

> *I can have sympathy, but apparently no empathy. So I find it very hard to imagine how something may feel for someone else. It's even hard for me to realise it for myself, what I feel and what it means. But I can't do it with someone else. So if I say something, I'm not going to think about how that person will feel if I say that. I often come across super brutish, and then people get angry with me and I don't know why.* [Robyn]

Attentiveness, a desire for quality, depth and a focus for details can also make a person very tired. Marie, for instance, describes how she sometimes focuses too much on details and fragments. This makes it very difficult for her to obtain an overall picture, which makes the world confusing:

> *'Being different' also means to me that I have found 'living' always so intensely difficult and complicated. The world is so confusing, it sometimes seems as if I see everything fragmented and then rapidly have to make an overall picture out of all those pieces and details, and this the whole day through.* [Marie]

For Baukis (60), diagnosed with autism at 58, the essence of autism is that information is processed in a different way. She gives an example from personal experience:

> *For me, that is the essence of autism: that you need much more time and energy to connect all loose particles of information and come to the right conclusion. I will give an example: I had little chicks in the garden, white to yellowish-brown in colour. There are also a lot of sparrows here who come for a little bite. One day, I'm on my terrace and I see a little light-coloured bird sitting outside the henhouse and I think: hey, a white sparrow? Later, I come to the conclusion that I was wrong, a white sparrow, that's not right. It was of course a little chick who must've climbed through the fence. Someone else would've probably recognised a chick much sooner.* [Baukis]

The difference in how she processes information lies in the fact that Baukis has trouble finding an overview in the details, connecting the loose particles to come to the right conclusion. Sofie describes how she sometimes concentrates so much on a particular issue that she misses other meaningful events:

> *Well, I don't know if I see more things than others but what I do know – because me and my partner always laugh about it – ... For instance, there was a new TV in the living room, but I needed something from the cupboard, so then I don't notice the new TV. I go straight for my goal and I ignore that TV completely, I don't see that. So do I see more? We also had to look at a photo of a kitchen scene, I only noticed those kitchen cabinets. So do you see more? No, on the contrary, I think you see much less.* [Sofie]

The fact that people care much about essences, more than about trivialities, also means that conventional or unimportant categories do not matter. For Els (47), diagnosed with autism a year before the interview, this also applies when she thinks about choosing a partner:

> *Indeed, when I look back and think about it, when I consider my circle of friends for instance and think about whom I feel more attracted to and whom I feel less attracted to, I absolutely don't discriminate between male or female, it is every time about what they say, what they do and who they are.* [Els]

Caring about essences is sometimes interpreted by others as a lack of imagination. In the quotation below, Vic (39)—diagnosed two times (in 2004 and in 2014)—refers to *The Neverending Story*, a film from the '1980s where a ten-year-old boy falls into a fantasy world after reading a book. One of the main characters is a large white dragon with a dog's head:

> *The thing is, if your own imagination is richer than the one such as Neverending Story makes, the story is very boring, right. I can't surpass the fact that I'm sitting in my comfy chair, watching that dragon or flying dog or whatever. I see fabric, I can't surpass that.* [Vic]

Vic himself, however, does not interpret this as a lack of imagination from his side, but he considers it to be a *surplus* of imagination: because of his imagination, he looks straight through the illusion raised by the filmmakers. He also explains this based on the literary writers he prefers:

> *I'm not a big fan of Tolkien for instance, but that is because... I quite prefer the concrete, in the way Coetzee can be concrete. He can for instance describe the*

bottom of a landscape and then I almost smell or taste the earth. Or in the case of 'Waiting for the Barbarians', *I get thirsty from the dry and dusty ground in that book. Murakami is okay, certainly, but a book with nothing but surrealistic Murakami situations, no thanks. That's why I prefer* Norwegian Wood *over* iq84. *And yes, I don't see myself as a little kid totally losing myself in a puppet show, shouting at little red riding hood that the wolf is hiding in a corner, and that she should be careful. I always looked behind that panel at the puppeteer, to observe him.* [Vic]

The fact that people with a diagnosis of autism often have a different sensory perception has been known for a long time. Still, 'sensory problems' were not mentioned in the description of autism until the DSM-5. In our interviews, it was striking how a more intense experience of sensory perceptions, for instance hypersensitivity to noise, was really felt as disturbing. Sofie explains:

Sofie: *Yes I become difficult, yes (laughs), very difficult. I get annoyed, I also always complain like, wow, those noisy people... Yeah...*
KH: *And can you say what it is about that noise that really bothers you? Does it make it impossible for you to think about anything else, does it make you tired?*
Sofie: *Uh, yeah, that dominates everything, and it comes in so heavily that I become difficult because of it. And bustle, I can't handle that either.*

Carl also describes how he—ever since he was a child—experienced disturbing noise, and a lot of it. Since no one wanted to believe him, he recorded this noise with a tape recorder when he was 14:

I also made a sound recording once, simply of the sounds during lunch. Yes, why do you do something like that? You can interpret it all afterwards, the sound was too much... But I also think, everyone has something he can be bothered about, yes, well there happened to be a lot of noise at home (laughs). But you can only know that when someone else also says like: "gee, there is a lot of noise here", you see? So for me that was normal. [Carl]

At the end of this quotation, Carl describes how impossible it is to know if something is 'objectively' too much noise, without checking this with others. How do you know if someone else also experiences a certain sound as noise? Recording sound is an attempt to allow someone else to distinguish and determine this 'too much'. Sandra also describes how she can be overstimulated by visual impressions:

> *Being overstimulated, gee, that's when I get too many impulses. For instance when I go somewhere and there are too many people. I am oversensitive to sounds, to impressions, to images, to everything. If I get overstimulated, it is as if my brain can't handle it anymore, can't filter anymore. I can be very stressed then, very flustered. This can also make me so tired.* [Sandra]

Later on in the conversation, Sandra describes how she became physically unwell at an office party:

> *For instance, two years ago, I just started working again, and I had to go to a New Year's reception. There were about 400, 500 people. I said to my boss: "Do I really have to go there, because I think it's not good for me, I know it's not good for me". He says: "Yes, you have to go, everyone is expected to be there". Okay so I go there, I go inside – it was in the factory in R, well, that is a very dark place. I went inside, there was this horrible band playing, with trumpets and such, and I think that is horrible. I see all those tables, I can still describe how that was, what stood where, the tables that stood there, the colour of the curtains, where the music was. And I see all those people and I hear everything, and all at once it seemed, but that sounds so weird, that I wasn't there anymore. I started walking around like a headless chicken and then I also couldn't talk. I literally became sick, just sick while I wasn't anxious or anything, right. But I just got sick because of all those impressions. And then at a certain moment I was just gone, I don't really remember it myself. Then my manager came and said: "Sandra are you all right?" I said: "No". I was gone again. I can't remember much more, until the moment that another boss asked me: "Sandra are you okay?" And I said: "No" and I started to cry and I must've gone like: "stop, stop, it hurts so much"… That was really because of the impressions for me, people thought that I panicked and that I cried because of the social aspect, but that had nothing to do with it. At that moment, that was just as if my ears – that's how it felt – were being ripped apart from the inside out. In the end I really didn't know anymore. They asked like: "What are you going to do?". I'm like: "I don't know". And then I was gone and my boss came and he said: "And now you're going home."* [Sandra]

Sandra describes her experience as an obvious, physical malaise, leading to physical nausea. She also uses the words 'pain' and 'despair'. Interestingly, this event dates back to when she had already been diagnosed with autism: her colleagues, who were aware of this diagnosis, interpret her panic as a result of an impossibility to hold her own in a social setting. Sandra, however, emphasises that what happened is indeed physical pain related to overstimulation.

In the next quotation, Bas describes how this sensory overstimulation complicates performing in a noisy work environment:

> *It is also that space, right, where that eternal radio is playing, which is a reason in itself why I can't do nine out of ten jobs. And if you dare to say something about that, you are public enemy number one.* [Bas]

Here too, there is a mismatch between the majority—who is not bothered by it and therefore also not tempted to do something about it—and the person who is unable to do his job because he is not allowed to turn the radio off. A bit further on, Bas describes how this overstimulation also complicates stepping out into the world:

> *It actually easily comes at you when you just leave the door at home, or even before that, and you step into the normal world and you mingle with the people. Even if you just go to the shop, there will also probably be a radio playing or something like that, and devices that make an insane amount of noise even. You can also ask questions about this regarding functionality. And then there is too much light everywhere, unpleasant smells,* etcetera. [Bas]

Not all participants are bothered by overstimulation to the same extent. Some of them experience moments when this occurs, and moments when this is no problem at all. Michael (26 at the time of the interview), diagnosed with autism and NLD since 2011, explains that it is not so bad for him:

> *I can stand quite a lot of stimulation, so it's not too bad. If it's too much, it's just mainly when they're ear stimuli. For instance, I can't concentrate when there is too much noise, but I can work in a little bit of noise. In that festivity hall where I work now, there* is *a lot of noise.* [Michael]

A recurring theme throughout the conversations is a strong feeling of justice and an aversion to injustice. Albert writes:

> *I can't stand people who lie or don't tell the truth. I can't stand injustice. If there is something I really can't stand, I get really angry and I feel frustrated. This makes me physically uncomfortable and very tired. During those moments, I prefer to crawl into my bed and sleep all day. I sometimes dare to do this.* [Albert]

When we ask Matteo about what he really cannot handle, he answers:

Certain kinds of peer pressure or something, that bothers me yes.... For instance in my football team when we have to do an exercise at the end of the training, I can actually handle that, but I can't handle it that they invent exercises that one or two people are the victims of.

The feeling of injustice can rise to such levels that it overwhelms the person and hinders his or her performance. Els explains that the fact that two of her colleagues had an affair was insurmountable for her:

I worked in a team with two colleagues. Those two had a secret relationship and were cheating on their partners and children. That didn't work for my autistic brain. [...] Now I realise that. This was terribly difficult for me. I had learned in my life that it is better to keep quiet about these things, but then the people of the secretariat would come to me and laugh about it and I would laugh along with them. But it was more forced than genuine. And they went home in the evening and laughed it off, but I didn't, I was stuck with it. I had to work with these people. They were together in one office the whole day, and if I had a question I had to wait until she went home and he had an hour to spare for me. He was also the manager of the team. But I just couldn't handle it, there was friction everywhere. So I decided to leave. [Els]

In two interviews (Marie and Mickey), the theme 'traffic' is addressed, and the annoyance when people do not follow traffic rules. Mickey describes how he always follows the traffic rules:

I know not everyone is as fast or as skilled, but I never drive too fast. If it says 90, you have to drive 90, or I drive 70 or I drive 50 or even 30 where it's allowed, where it's obliged. [Mickey]

BartDelam also says he always found it difficult when people did not follow the rules. He describes how he can get very angry when someone parks in front of a garage: before his diagnosis, this was incomprehensible and insurmountable. In Chap. 5 (*Autism as a Way to Hold Your Own*), we will come back to how the diagnosis has enabled him to get over this in the end.

Deficits in social interaction is one of the criteria for the diagnosis of autism, as defined in DSM-5. Our respondents indeed describe how they sometimes have difficulties in social situations. They, however, often ascribe possible problems to the fact that they have problems with superficiality, or with small talk. This can, for instance, lead to problems at work, as Bas describes:

> *And then I want to talk about substance at work, and about procedures, and actually about: how we can make everything as good and as agreeable as possible. But it seems my colleagues or bosses only want to chitchat about everything, except about what it is actually about: that work. They care more about your non-verbal appearance.* [Bas]

The theme of having problems with small talk comes back in several conversations. Albert describes it as follows:

> *I don't intuitively sense people. What do they like to talk about? Are they open to a conversation? Do they think I'm cool/interesting enough to talk to or are they just polite? It is difficult for me to start a conversation and keep it going. I think small talk is useless, insincere and superficial. I am for instance not interested in where someone went for their holiday. Do people think this is an interesting thing to know about me? I think that other people can do this all automatically, without asking themselves questions.* [Albert]

Marie says:

> *The chitchat about the weather in the elevator, small talk etc. Is that really necessary? Are people perhaps afraid of silences that every wordless moment has to be filled with 'verbal diarrhoea', as I call it....?!* [Marie]

She further explains how problems in communication are often due to a combination of events:

> *I do think that it's important to be the same to a certain extent – 'to a certain extent', because after all, we are all unique. An example: when you are somewhere for the first time, and people ask: "Were you able to find it?", I'm flabbergasted. I also used to struggle with the 'it' – by now I know that people are talking about the location or the address – but would I have walked in if I HADN'T been able to find it, huh?!! Confusing! People should know what such a simple question triggers inside my brain: Find what? Did I have to find something?? Oh, he means if I was able to find this location! Well I'm here, aren't I, he can see that too, why does he ask? Am I late perhaps? Check watch. No, in time... Oh shoot! I hope my watch isn't wrong! Must look at it later. Is there a clock somewhere? And so it goes, on and on... Just add a handshake (=tactile*

sense) with an unknown person, in a strange environment with loads of new impressions (=hear, see, smell) and I practically fall over from exhaustion, even before the conversation really starts. [Marie]

The substantive level of a conversation is important, but a number of participants have learned through trial and error that the majority of the people is not very interested in deep conversations, or that people say things that have more to do with convention than substance. Bluetopian says:

A lot of people – most of them – don't want to hurt you and start to describe things more carefully, formulate their answers more prudently. They say for instance: "I'll speak to you about it one of the following days". But actually they don't want to talk about it ever again. To tone this down, it becomes: "I'll speak to you about it one of the following days." If I say: "we'll speak about it one of the following days, I will (generally) do this. [Bluetopian]

The inability to engage in small talk is often combined with a penchant for real conversations. Hannah (36) received her diagnosis when she was 34. She shares how she dreads spending the evening on the neighbours' terrace, because there she will have to chitchat. She finds it horrendous. She also thinks that people often think she is too serious. Still, she notices that her ability to have deep conversations is appreciated by a number of people:

Yeah, they'll say like – there's not many of them right, there are only a few who I can really do that with – and they say: "Oh you speak so naturally about the most difficult things and yes, we can talk to you about things we can never talk about with other people". That is the response I get, and yes that I talk about it in a very normal way while other people are like, we're not going to talk about that subject. While I maybe sometimes ask for it a bit too much, but people don't mind then, because they say: "oh we can have a deep conversation with you the whole evening, and it doesn't stop and then it's 2 AM all of a sudden and then we actually wish it wasn't over yet." [Hannah]

Others also explain that they have some good friends with whom they can have deep conversations. Marie says that she likes to have face-to-face conversations. The feeling of being on the same wavelength makes her feel less lonely. This is not really the case when she has to talk in group, and throughout the interview she makes it clear that she actually thinks group conversations are horrible. The fact that she was encouraged to do this during a long stay in the psychiatric hospital, and that they didn't take her aversion of this into account, still makes her angry:

> *I think a good conversation with a friend is always nice: face-to-face moments – without a third or fourth person present, so purely one-on-one – and being able to talk freely about stuff without feeling embarrassed or having to hold back. I happen to be so lucky that I have known my best friend for more than 30 years: we have been through a lot together and feel more like sisters than friends. I especially love the closeness, the connectedness, being on the same wavelength. I suspect this is because of the fact that I have always had the feeling that I didn't belong, so when I have a real good conversation with a friend, I can really enjoy it.* [Marie]

ASSpirin also describes how she hates small talk. She does sometimes have deep conversations with other people. She gives the example of a conversation with a lady whom she met through a 'give away-site' on the internet. She describes the contact to be "to the point, deep, a reciprocity and openness".

Our respondents report on how they often felt different than others. They have the feeling that they react differently than others, and perceive differently, sometimes experience things sharper, and sometimes are more absent. Other perceptions—for instance visual, auditive or tactile stimuli— are the subject of Ashley E. Robertson and David R. Simmons' study, a focus group-study of six adults with a diagnosis of autism. The study showed that an excess of stimuli can cause physical pain.[2] The feeling of 'being different' has also been described in other studies, such as Jones, Zahl and Huws' *First-hand Account of Emotional Experiences in Autism: a Quantitative Analysis*, where the authors analyse Internet reports of five people who identified themselves as 'highly functioning'.[3] They were of the opinion that these people exemplified a feeling of being different, of not belonging to this planet. This leads to frustration and often also to periods of depression and feelings of fear and discomfort. For our respondents, feeling different leads to a search for and wanting to know who one really is. People want an answer to the question "how will I ever be able to hold my own"? Our study enables us to substantiate the opinion that being different or feeling different has an impact on mental well-being. In the next chapter, this will be further explored.

[2] Robertson, David and Simmons (2015).
[3] Jones, Zahl and Huws (2001).

BIBLIOGRAPHY

Frith, Uta. 2003. *Autism: Explaining the Enigma*. 2nd ed. Malden: Blackwell Pub.

Jones, R.S.P., A. Zahl, and J.C. Huws. 2001. First-Hand Accounts of Emotional Experiences in Autism: A qualitative analysis. *Disability & Society* 16 (3): 393–401.

Robertson, A.E., R. David, and R. Simmons. 2015. The Sensory Experiences of Adults with Autism Spectrum Disorder: A Qualitative Analysis. *Perception* 44 (5): 569–586.

CHAPTER 3

Perspectives on Suffering

Abstract Many interviewees have always known that they were different and have certainly had their share of misery due to misunderstandings and not fitting in. Some already had their suspicions that they might have autism; for others, the diagnosis came as a surprise. The respondents explain how living in modern-day society is hard for them and sometimes very demanding. They tell us how functioning in this set reality exhausts them, how demanding the pressure from society is and how lonely they sometimes feel. An important element of this chapter is that it illustrates our interviewees' desire for human contact and communication.

Keywords Autism • Challenges • Suffering • Diagnosis • Adulthood

© The Author(s) 2018
K. Hens, R. Langenberg, *Experiences of Adults Following an Autism Diagnosis*, https://doi.org/10.1007/978-3-319-97973-1_3

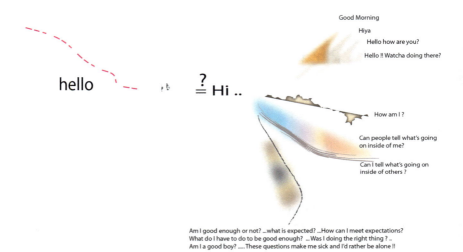

Being different can cause confrontations, feelings of isolation and difficulty understanding the people around you. Some interviewees were fortunate enough to have people in their immediate surroundings that took up a type of protective role, which provided just enough compensation to enable them to function in society. Others followed a developmental path which enabled them to avoid certain confrontations. And then others describe how they sometimes have an extreme reaction to events which most people find bearable. Still, all the respondents recall moments in their lives when it became too much, when things turned out badly for them.

Although for some respondents the diagnosis of autism was unexpected, it seems as if overall, there was simply no way around evolving towards a diagnosis. When confronted with their immediate surroundings, they were continuously reminded of how different they were from others. Justified doubt about the reasonability of their own experiences, ways of thinking and reactions is a constant factor, and in some cases develops into a fear of simply existing. Almost all interviewees decided to undergo a diagnostic session after a very difficult period in their lives, because they experienced external pressure to such an extent that they were no longer able to continue in the same way. In this chapter, we will focus on the parts of the interviews that describe these difficulties.

It seems as if the feeling of 'being different' as described in the previous chapter leads to problems at a certain point. However, as long as you are not asked to account for it as a child or as an adult, the problem is non-existent. Tatiana—who was diagnosed after battling a depression—says her feeling of being different as a child was also due to the fact that she grew up as the daughter of a local vet in the countryside, where the other children (farmer's daughters) did not share her interests. Tatiana enjoyed collecting stamps, studying maps and so forth. If she had known children who had had the same interests as her, the feeling might have been less pressing. Another story comes from Els, who had a very sheltered upbringing. The problems first presented themselves when she found herself in an extremely difficult working environment:

> *Yes I read that most people are diagnosed when they're adults, when their children are diagnosed, when they encounter problems at work or when they have children. In other words, when your life becomes too busy. Too much stress. With me, that didn't happen because of my strong family network I guess. My children have also sometimes been a source of stress, but not excessively. I had work, a career, and my parents and my in-laws took it in turns to pick the children up from school. The children could come home peacefully after school, they could do their homework, they got an afternoon snack and if I was late, dinner would be prepared, always around six.* [Els]

Els was diagnosed after three years of treatment by a psychologist, who eventually did not know what to do with her anymore. Bullying by a supervisor at work had caused her to break down and she attempted suicide. Before all this, her life had always had a structured and protected course; she was a top student at school and got high grades at university. We find a similar story with Kris (45), who was diagnosed four months before the interview. He explains how he had a sheltered upbringing, with a well-defined structure within his family:

> *But yes all my life I have had the feeling that I'm different than others, and yes, there have also been several incidents. Until I was 12, I did have a structured family, my parents and my sister and everything was nicely organised. In the diagnostic study, they also noticed and determined that my parents – without realising it – always compensated for what I could have difficulty with, or what I struggled with.* [Kris]

Even though he always felt different, Kris explains how the problems really started in the final years of secondary school and the first years of higher education, since part of the structure that was present during his childhood and puberty was no longer there. In 2008, Kris already suspected he met the diagnostic criteria for autism, but he faced resistance from his psychiatrist. He was of the opinion that Kris, because of his higher education, steady job, strong verbal capacity and his lack of specific physical characteristics of autism, did not fit the picture. Kris recently had himself tested, as a result of his divorce:

> I already had a suspicion in 2008, but it was actually moved aside by both psychiatrist and psychologist because I'm very high functioning and I have a university degree, Master of communication sciences. I'm also an educated social assistant, option social-cultural work, so I have an additional degree in social studies. I work fulltime and I have a high-ranking official position. [...]
>
> The fact that I was always very able to adapt to all kinds of circumstances, was able to develop a lot of coping strategies, played the chameleon a lot, have always tried to meet other people's wishes, I always kind of slipped through, so to speak. This is why the autism has only now, under my direction actually, been effectively diagnosed. But I had already experienced periods of serious depressions, often after relationship problems, heavy breakups. So there have been quite some signals. I have also always had that feeling like "I'm different than others" and searched for a long time what it could be. In 2008, after a heavy depression and a breakup, I actually really started to search for "what is this with me? Now I want to know". I crawled behind my laptop and pc and looked up everything I could find on the internet, and then pretty soon I got to the conclusion… by reading about it and facing it, I identified tremendously with what was called Asperger's syndrome at the time, what now – in general terms – is called autism spectrum disorder in DSM-5. Anyway, it was really pushed off the table by the psychiatrist that treated me, who told me: "You, that can't be, that's impossible". This is of course the pitfall for a certain group of autistic people who indeed function very highly, but with respect to suffering, with respect to problems from within, experience the same issues all autistic people experience. I really did suffer a lot, yes. [Kris]

Our respondents describe how, in their lives before the diagnosis, they often had the feeling they could not hold their own under both external and internal pressures. Bluetopian had himself tested in 2015 after his psychologist expressed the suspicion that he might have Asperger's. He had already experienced several years of mental suffering. He writes about his unstoppable train of thought: "Where is the off-button? There isn't one. It goes on and on… That's really exhausting…" With this, Bluetopian expresses the idea that thoughts can no longer be suppressed. Robyn had herself tested more recently, also after her psychiatrist suggested it. After a suicide attempt when she was 12, Robyn ended up in adult psychiatry, where her autism was not recognised. Robyn describes a similar experience and calls it a *train of thoughts*:

> But for instance, if I receive a message from a friend – yes I really have a TGV[1] of thoughts, that's extremely exhausting, too – but with me, they have been able to prove it in the tests, that my processing speed is very high. So that really means it's flash flash flash flash flash and that's how it is. And I also notice it, that when I get such a message, then it starts with me like: "yes but what does she actually mean with that, does she want to say it like this or like that, is it based on that, did I do that wrong…" [Robyn]

Robyn describes here how her thoughts dominate her, how she thinks things through too far, which is very exhausting in itself. She furthermore explains how her friends sometimes can't follow that, and how that leads to misunderstandings since she has thought out too many connections, while her friends have not yet reached that conclusion.

A few interviewees describe the tendency to dwell on certain things too long and too deeply. This often leads to incomprehension on the employers' side and an impossibility to move forward. People are faced with a world wherein everything is expected to accelerate constantly. The next quotation illustrates how Bas has problems with the demands from the outside world, for instance that certain imperfections should be overlooked. Bas himself suspected he had autism for a long time and had himself tested recently. He describes how his desire to stick to content leads to conflicts:

> I always say: if I had smiled a bit more now and then, and chatted along a bit, I wouldn't have gotten into trouble. If you're at work every week with your issues like "The way we are doing it now, why don't we do this or that", you make yourself extremely unpopular apparently, while you're saying it all in a good cause. Apparently it doesn't always go over well, both with the colleagues and the bosses. Sooner or later, it becomes a bomb and the other will fire me, right. It basically doesn't happen the other way around. [Bas]

---

[1] Train Grande Vitesse (fr), or high-speed train.

Many respondents describe difficult periods, either right before the diagnosis or throughout their entire life. Samuel was already diagnosed with autism combined with mental disability when he was five years old. He is also epileptic. Samuel has several degrees in higher education, and when he was 30—after a depression—he was diagnosed again. Michael's ASD and *Non-verbal Learning Disorder* (NLD) diagnoses came after a stay in a psychiatric hospital because of a burnout (he worked in a bakery where he had to work more than 60 hours a week).

For a few interviewees, the suggestion that they would have autism was quite unexpected; for others, it was something they themselves already knew, for instance, because they had children with a similar diagnosis. Sofie had already had herself tested eight years ago because she suspected she had autism, but the test was negative then. Her son was diagnosed with Asperger's syndrome and after taking a course for parents of children with autism, she recently had herself retested. ASSpirin identified with the description of autism when she trained to be a nurse seven years ago. After her niece's diagnosis, she ended up with the Flemish Autism Association (*Vlaamse Vereniging Autisme* [*VVA*]). There, she spoke with a woman who had autism, whose story she immediately recognised.

Albert had himself tested on the recommendation of a psychiatrist whom he visited because of depression. His son was diagnosed with autism, but the suggestion that this diagnosis also applied to him came as a surprise:

> Due to a heavy depression and concern from my partner and my son's psychologist (who's ASD was not yet determined at that time), I ended up with a psychiatrist. During our first conversation, she'd already mentioned she suspected it to be ASD. My wife and I were completely taken aback. I wanted to see proof first through further examination. [Albert]

For Robyn, the diagnosis also came as a surprise. She was a bit reluctant at first as well, given the fact that she had already been diagnosed several times with several disorders ever since she was young: generalised anxiety disorder, borderline personality disorder and schizotypal personality disorder:

> I actually went to the psychiatrist for a different reason, and he has... After two-three conversations he was like: "Yeah, I think I would like to have you tested for autism." I really laughed at him, I remember it very well. Like yeah, how did you get to that. Like, don't I have enough labels already, gee. [Robyn]

A bit later, Robyn explains that she connected the syndrome of Asperger to Kim de Gelder, the young man who stabbed and killed several children and carers in a Nursery in Dendermonde in 2009. After the tests and the appropriate explanations, however, she completely agreed with her diagnosis.

A few of the participants experience certain aspects of modern life, such as computers or telephones, as problematic because these technologies cause extra pressure. Hannah has been a teacher for a while and identified with the descriptions of autism when she read about the topic for her job. She also always felt different, and her partner agreed that there could be something else going on with her. She describes how it is difficult for her to find peace in modern life:

> *Now everyone has to participate in that busy life, and a lot more people experience just how heavy that extra pressure is. And then it comes more to the surface, because if I for instance, when I went to uni it was much less for me, that pressure. Because I had – that was just before the big computer and internet era – so I also didn't have a computer in my room or something. So I found a lot of peace there, and because I found it I was also a lot less panicky and I had less negative effects of autism because I had to deal with it less. And that became stronger when I started working.* [Hannah]

Throughout this interview, it becomes clear that Hannah experienced her time at the university as very pleasant. She links this to the fact that at that time, she was able to fully focus on a subject of her own choice, and she could generally interact with people with similar interests. Bas makes a similar remark about the problems in this day and age. Phone calls are problematic for him, and he thinks life would have been much easier if he had lived one or two centuries ago. Further on in the interview, he also mentions a fascination for the Scottish Highlands, which symbolise peace for him:

> *A telephone for instance, just the medium. I would have been much happier if it just hadn't been invented. I actually have the same opinion about almost all telecommunication. If I just would have been born a century or two ago, life would have been so much more agreeable, I think. If you arrived at work in those days, there would just be letters waiting for you, that's fantastic. I would give a lot to go back to such a situation.* [Bas]

Tatiana also describes how she considers the current communication tools such as emails to be too transient. She often finds herself writing emails that others consider to be too long. She needs that margin, however, to be able to write down what she actually wants to say, and she explains that this is why she sometimes yearns for the old-fashioned letter.

Another kind of pressure people experience is the pressure to meet an ideal image that eventually appears to be unattainable. Baukis was diagnosed at a later age, she was already 58. Because of an eating disorder, she spent a few months in a mental hospital as a young girl of 16. All three of her sons, 20 somethings, have been diagnosed with autism. She worked as a volunteer for the VVA and noticed that she had an increasing amount of things in common with women with autism. Raised in a catholic family that highly valued being a good and wholesome catholic, Baukis always had to contend with an ideal image she could not live up to:

> *Wanting to be a good catholic, that's actually not so easy in reality. The older I got, the more mistakes I made against that ideal image. Answering to those high values became more and more complicated, and the discrepancy between my ideal image and the realistic image grew bigger and bigger. Eventually, it tears you apart.* [Baukis]

A few respondents express the feeling that the more they try, the worse it gets. In the long quotation below, Tatiana describes how she finds it very difficult to plan practical things and bring them to a good end. She illustrates this by telling a story about how her focus on detail had a large impact on the bigger picture:

> *So I am always concerned with doing it right and then I make a mistake. That happened as well, not so long ago in Sardinia. I had booked a flight, back to the Netherlands, and had to go from one side of the island to the other side to get there. But there in Sardinia the public transport is tremendously bad. And I had no money at all, and on holiday everything has to be as cheap as possible. We couldn't do anything there because we had no money. And then I had to find out how we could get to the airport in time, that day and with that much luggage.*
> *[…]*
> *I was so tense then and thinking that it couldn't go wrong. I had really worked it all out very well, I specifically went to the station because it isn't all on the internet. I went to the station, took pictures, the trips to that city where the airport is. There was only one train in the morning, we had to have it, that was at seven o'clock. I memorised that very well, I stayed awake all night, called*

> the taxi, at half past six, the station is nearby, all went well. I stayed up all night and my husband too so we wouldn't be too late. Then we arrived at the station and went to buy tickets. And then they said that I could validate the tickets in an hour and a half. I say: "yes but the train leaves in about ten minutes." They reply: "no, in an hour and a half." I say: "no in about ten minutes." Turns out the train had already left at six. We couldn't catch it anymore. Yes then we had to take a cab for about 200 euros. I had to pay it, but we did so little during our holiday because we had no money, and then my husband was really very angry. And those kinds of things happen almost every day. [Tatiana]

This quotation illustrates that she, just by trying to do everything right because it is so important, does not see what is happening, that her initial assumption is wrong. By starting from untested hypotheses, then blindly following that track and not connecting it to reality, Tatiana gets in trouble.

Some of the participants describe how they feel that they have no boundaries, which makes them want to go too far. They have trouble laying down a type of structure or rules in their lives that would enable them to sense when something is supposed to happen. A few participants describe how difficult it is for them to implement a healthy sleeping pattern:

> I theoretically know perfectly well what sleeping hygiene is: going to bed in time, turning the TV off, getting stimuli-free, unwinding, drinking a cup of tea, going for a little walk… Rationally, I know very well what I am supposed to do, but I can't. But I already have this for twenty, twenty-five, thirty years, so since I left my parents' home, that in the evening I become more active the later it gets, can be very focused like yesterday, when I'm looking up info on triathlon. There, another article and another one, ah start to swim and start to triathlon, and that's two, three, four o'clock at night. So that's something I have a lot of problems with, to create enough sleep. Well that has been going on for months. If it goes on like this, I will probably crash again because with three hours of sleep a night I'm not going to make it. [Kris]

Kris describes how he, although he knows rationally that he needs more sleep, and also knows what he has to do to get it, still is not able to do it. Tatiana explains how she writes long emails to her employer until the early hours of the night, and actually realises that the employer in question does not appreciate this at all. Still, she often relapses into this pattern. Mickey also speaks about how impossible it is for him to stop doing a certain activity:

> *I rarely interrupt an activity. If I'm doing something, I want to do that forever, that's the ideology behind it. That is why I don't really have a problem with overtime. When I'm working I just want to keep working, I'm in that mode anyway. When I'm on my PlayStation I want to keep playing with my PlayStation. When I'm sleeping, I want to continue sleeping. When I'm awake, I want to stay awake, that's why I'm awake until two at night, just because I don't want to go to sleep, because I feel that the day can't be over yet...* [Mickey]

Mickey describes it as a 'mode', and refers to a period of intense concentration on something specific, for instance his work (as a welder) or gaming on his PlayStation. It is almost impossible for him to stop it, which leads to sleep deprivation.

The previous quotations illustrate that the respondents often suffer, and specifically experience many and long-lasting insecurities concerning their person, and how to participate in life. All our respondents have sought for help to find more clarity about themselves. The initiative to get tested came from the participants themselves, from their partners or from a psychiatrist. Some of them were recently divorced or decided to get tested because of the strain on their relationship. Carl, for instance, had himself tested after a long period of conflict and after his then-wife—who suspected Carl might have Asperger's—suggested it to him. With Matteo, it was his father—a history teacher—and his sisters, who in 2007, after periods of ongoing arguments, suggested he should have himself examined for Asperger's syndrome. Tatiana describes how she experienced a very difficult period after her parents passed away and after she separated from her previous husband and lost a lot of her friends:

> *I have been through some hard times: my parents passed away, I went through a very nasty divorce and lost everything. And then I ended up in a very different social, spiritual position or something. I lost all of my friends, and at that moment I had already very much accepted that loss, and now they're slowly coming back to me. But I already processed the loss, or at least, I have already accepted it. So yes, if they come back or not, if they do come back it's nice, but I'm not going to try as hard as I used to. If they don't come back I have accepted it anyway.* [Tatiana]

Mickey had himself tested after his wife recommended it, although he already suspected as much, also because his brother has a similar diagnosis:

> *Technically, yes, but the suspicion has always been there. I have never had the intention to get myself tested. I was afraid perhaps, I don't know… my wife also wanted to know for if we were to make children, because it's hereditary.* [Mickey]

But he also sensed that at a certain point, it became impossible to continue working at the same pace:

> *Yes, I really worked there up until the point I became unwell. I had to throw up because of the stress and I stayed home for five weeks. I then started working again at a slower pace, but that pace was increased immediately. And then, I had a temporary fixed contract so I couldn't hand in my notice. I had to work there until the beginning of September, but I agreed with them, I had made an agreement that I wanted to quit sooner. That has to happen in agreement with the boss, and they finally agreed with the 1st of August.* [Mickey]

Our respondents often mention the tension between the desire for contact with others on the one hand and problems to maintain this contact on the other hand. For some, this went hand in hand with a feeling of loneliness, as Tatiana says: "I love the people very much but I just can't maintain the contact. I think that's very sad because I'm quite lonely." In the next quotation, Bluetopian describes how he suffers a great deal from that loneliness:

> *Loneliness is an understatement for me. I suffer a great deal. So yeah, there is a difference with what's 'mainstream'. Do I really have to be 'mainstream'? No, not at all. But I belong to the category of autists who do need social contacts. Establishing – and particularly maintaining – those social contacts is disturbed. This leads to great loneliness, which causes a great level of suffering.* [Bluetopian]

Here, Bluetopian opposes the thought that all autists are supposedly people who don't need contacts, and refers specifically to different 'kinds' of autists. He also refers to the fact that this loneliness is existential, which implies that such a loneliness is very difficult to prevent and is more than a simple lack of contact. Throughout the conversation, it also becomes clear that Bluetopian felt this loneliness both before and after the diagnosis. Contact with other autists does not necessarily mean that he feels less lonely: "Even within the world of autism, I feel the odd one out… very painful!"

Loneliness is also related to the feeling of being an outsider, something that causes a lot of suffering. In the quotations below, Kris describes his attempts to fit in and how he never really succeeded:

> *A nice word I learned the past weeks is 'level of suffering'. I really suffered from it, especially because I didn't feel at home with others. Even though I'm present amongst others, I will still feel alone there. That is also something which often comes back: that I feel as if I'm not included in a group, even if you are physically included or even mentally or whatever. But still never having that feeling and always feeling that you're the outsider, yes that feeling has always been present very strongly....*
>
> *[...]*
>
> *I never really fully felt at home, I was with a football club but okay I played along and all and tried to go along as much as possible with that group process. And yet I always felt the outsider. I have always felt to be the outsider, also at work, and also with friends: like never really being able to connect, like never really belonging to the group.* [Kris]

Other respondents felt the loneliness much less. BartDelam ended up in depression caused by exhaustion in 2012, which was the reason for him to get tested. For a long time, he suspected he could be autistic, even though he also had his doubts. During his work as a social nurse, he mostly came into contact with people who also had a mental disability, besides autism. He did not really identify with their situation. BartDelam describes that he has less need for contact with people than others do, and that he also does not really miss people:

> *Thanks to my girlfriend, and thanks to my ex-wife before, I have a lot of social contacts. Sometimes too many, because I actually have little desire for it and it often feels like a social obligation. The initiative for social contacts hardly ever comes from me. If I was alone, I would very rarely contact others. The degree of connectedness with others is hard to measure, but should the people around me die, there are very few of them I would really miss.* [BartDelam]

Even though BartDelam somehow realises that others consider it to be normal that you need people around you, and to miss them when they are not there, he does not sense that himself. He describes it as "a different feeling of connectedness".

One of the questions we asked during the interview was if the respondents were worried sometimes, and what they would worry about. We noticed that many of them answered "about everything". They were worried about the world, about loved ones, about themselves, about changes, about unpredictable events....

Vic was diagnosed with autism at two different times, both times when he was hospitalised due to psychoses. He describes how he completely panics when he loses overview. He is often not able to effectively do what he had planned to do that day:

> *I panic when I lose overview... When I don't feel well-prepared or when I'm not well rested because of circumstances. When I'm not well rested there is a real risk, then it's as if my brain is only switched on for 50%. Then it's precisely as if that side is lame, tame, or not there. Then it starts with like some sort of dead end street and it always becomes... But yeah and then... Then it is very difficult to like, when there's something wrong from the start, I have a very hard time the rest of the day...* [Vic]

He furthermore explains how a single event can mess up his entire plan:

> *No, no I can't let it go. It can also just be something physical right, because I'm too tired, I get dressed too slowly when I have an appointment which means I have to hurry all of a sudden and then... It can be little things right, it can be that I forgot to put my ring on. That's a disaster for me. Then I find out when I'm on the train and then not even one third of my day has passed, but then my day is... And then I hold my breath, because yeah...* [Vic]

For a few of the interviewees, concern is an overpowering feeling with far-reaching consequences. In Hannah's quotation below, the extent of her worries and anxiety become clear:

> *Now? About everything... Yeah really about everything. I'm a very fearful person. I'm also working with a coach, an auti-coach, and he tries to give me a bit of guidance with it. He says that my most important, or my biggest problem, is fear. That I continuously live in fear. And that I'm maybe not aware of it, but that it's my thoughts running wild. He tries to teach me a bit that it's like a radio playing and that I have to search for the off or exit button to find a bit of peace. Yeah I really worry about everything. This life is actually too heavy for me. I don't really know how I can say it differently than that I worry about everything, and about everyone and about how the whole world, and, yeah... I also have to, I also notice, I have also learned it throughout the years, I also have a great concern about the world and how everything happens in the world and the people in the world. When I was a child, I used to give all my savings to*

> Broederlijk Delen[2] *and now I just decided to no longer watch the news. I also don't watch unpleasant movies, I don't watch things about the Holocaust or things from Africa because I just can't handle it anymore.* [Hannah]

Hannah describes how she absorbs all the suffering in the world without distinction, which causes her life to become too heavy and results in her having to shut herself off from all these impressions. A few participants take medication to supress their anxieties. Sandra has two children diagnosed with autism. A couple of years before the interview, she checked herself into a mental hospital because of depression, she was in constant pain because of a disease but could not take any medication because of an allergy. During that stay, she was diagnosed with autism. She explains that her fears and worries also have to do with a fear of change:

> *I'm someone who's always worried. But for me it's not really worrying. Its rather something like: what's going to happen, the unexpected, the unknown. Is that being worried? No, for me that's not just simply being worried.* [Sandra]

Sandra describes how her fear for the unknown can no longer be regarded as merely 'being worried'. Kris also talks about his fear of the unknown:

> *For instance, if I go to a seminar for work, it's always something very fearsome for me. Then I think, yeah, where is it and where do I have to go in and who is going to be there and where am I going to sit? That's always quite a task for me.* [Kris]

Marie was admitted to the psychiatric hospital for a few months in 2007, in the department of personality disorders. There, she was diagnosed with borderline personality disorder, and she was encouraged to follow various therapies, including group therapy, which she did not experience as healing at all. When she left, she felt even worse. So bad even that she did not want to live anymore and her suffering had become unbearable. This made her decide to apply for euthanasia. During this application process, the psychiatrist who was part of the team assessing whether or not her suffering was unbearable enough to qualify for euthanasia suggested that Marie should get herself tested for autism. Below, she describes how all-encompassing that fear for change—also in herself—can be:

---

[2] A Flemish organisation for development aid.

> *There are also the fears that I fall prey to on a daily basis: fear of change, of the unpredictable, the unknown, the uncontrollable. Fear to meet someone (known or unknown) unexpectedly. Furthermore, I am also afraid to lose knowledge, to disintegrate completely and lose myself. And then I haven't even mentioned the fear of the despair and sorrow that seem to devour me. Or fear of incomprehension when I try to explain my invisible suffering...* [Marie]

Besides an almost unbearable fear, also of her own suffering, Marie is also afraid of the fact that she can share this suffering with only a handful of people.

A number of participants had—long before we had had our conversation with them—already considered or even attempted suicide. There is Robyn, who tried to kill herself when she was 12, which caused her to spend her entire youth in psychiatric institutions and which prevented her from going to school. She graduated middle school through the examination board. The reason for her suicide attempt was the combination of a sudden change from a village school to a large middle school and discovering her being different. Baukis also undertook a suicide attempt when she was a young girl. And then there is Els, who could not bear the bullying at work anymore at a certain moment and considered suicide.

Nora (28) was diagnosed at 21. During her first year at a dancing school, she went through a very difficult period and ended up in a depression. Nora describes how she sometimes fantasised about suicide as a possible way out, but no longer considers it, the fantasy is enough:

> *Even though I'm quite optimistic, I'm very bothered by what they call 'black thoughts'. It's some sort of joy of life that's missing. Ever since I was 6 years old, I've had a strong death wish, and even though the concreteness of that wish is not particularly present, thinking about 'not having to live anymore' has become some sort of escape mechanism during difficult moments. I can talk about that with some people, which keeps it 'safe' time after time. But it never goes away. Even if I have very good moments, filled with joy, it often flashes through my head that now, during such a blissful moment, it would be good if it all ended. Then all worries would be over and there would be peace.* [Nora]

In Belgium, it is possible to request euthanasia because of unbearable psychological suffering.[3] This is possible if it can be proven that the suffering is hopeless, continuous and unbearable. You must be an adult, and several

---
[3] Thienpont (2017).

doctors have to be involved in the advice. Below, Marie further explains what she experienced after her stay in a mental hospital:

> *When I left the mental hospital nine months later, I was 500% convinced that I didn't belong on this planet and I had learned even better to live with a mask on. They told me I would experience recognition and acknowledgement in a group. The only thing I found there was total confusion, superficiality (because I didn't dare show myself), annoyance with regard to the absurd therapies that appeared completely futile to me, plus also misunderstanding from doctors and nursing staff. Luckily, my depression had improved thanks to the medication and a fellow patient – who became a good friend – pulled me through that rough period.* [Marie]

When she was eventually dismissed from the psychiatric hospital, she felt that no one could help her, and that her situation was hopeless. After discussion with her partner, she filed an application for euthanasia:

> *It didn't go well: apparently I couldn't survive without medication and when autumn came, my suicide plans became very concrete again. As I saw it, I was out of options: given my experience with psychiatry, another admission was absolutely impossible. I had already tried therapy so often (with psychiatrists and psychologists), I didn't want any more narcotics and medication meant side effects (such as weight gain with back problems as a consequence). When I discussed with my girlfriend that I seriously considered suicide, she begged me to not suddenly kill myself but to do it in a serene and soft way. Mid-October 2015 I handed in my request for euthanasia because of unbearable mental suffering.* [Marie]

After her diagnosis, Marie decides she first wants to work on that before she continues with the euthanasia process. Marie's story is an angry story about how mental healthcare has dealt with her problems. During her stay in the mental hospital, she was solely tested for personality disorders. If she had also been tested for a developmental disorder, she would have been diagnosed with autism a lot sooner. Her therapeutic path would have been completely different and people might even have had more understanding for the fact that group therapy was not helping her. Baukis also describes that the time she spent in the psychiatric hospital when she was 16 has done her more harm than good:

> *I'll never forget the moment when I was brought into the mental hospital, it is engraved in my memory. That was where now the Bijloke museum[4] is and the*

---

[4] A museum in Ghent, Belgium.

current conservatory. The psychiatric ward was underground, room 14–15. You went through some sort of lock, the door behind you shut, locked. I had to take off my clothes and hand over my identity papers. Again through a door, which again shut behind me. I realised then that I – without clothing and without papers – couldn't get away anymore. I was 16 years old then. I stood in a big room where there was no daylight, nothing. On both sides of the room a row of beds with people everywhere, lying and hanging there expressionless. Am I like that, for people to bring me here? Will I become like that? Well, then the light goes out in your head, that's really horrible. And that my parents brought me there and left me there, that was the worst of all. [Baukis]

Baukis experienced her stay in the mental hospital as a punishment, which made the ideal image she so desperately tried to meet, even more unattainable.

Our respondents describe the problems and the suffering they experienced throughout their lives. They describe a profound fatigue, which they explain by referring to the rush of everyday life, but also to their own thoughts, which go on and on and on. They are often burdened by perfectionism, which makes the impossibility to meet an ideal image the cause of much suffering. They describe many fears: the fear of loneliness, the fear of conflicts with the people around them, the fear to lose overview or the fear of unpredictability. Also, a fear of negative reports from all over the world. The feeling of fear has also been studied by Trembath and colleagues in their paper *The Experience of Anxiety in Young Adults with Autism Spectrum Disorder*. Using two focus groups, one with adults between 18 and 35 years old diagnosed with autism, and one with professionals and parents of adults with autism, they investigate how autistic people experience anxieties, what the causes and consequences are, and how people deal with this. They also report the not understanding of what is expected in social situations, the loss of control when unpredictable events occur and a broader concern about other people's fate and the world in general as primary causes of fears.[5] In the next chapter, we will further examine the diagnostic process and the interviewees' experience of being tested.

---

[5] Trembath et al. (2012).

Bibliography

Thienpont, Lieve. 2017. *De pijn van anders zijn*. Gent: Academia Press.

Trembath, D., C. Germano, G. Johanson, and C. Dissanayake. 2012. The Experience of Anxiety in Young Adults with Autism Spectrum Disorders. *Focus on Autism and Other Developmental Disabilities* 27 (4): 213–224.

CHAPTER 4

The Experience of Being Tested

Abstract This chapter explores the different tests that are available to test for autism and lets the respondents explain what their experience was with these tests. Some respondents were very happy with the tests, others were more sceptical. Many respondents have already had different diagnoses before their autism diagnosis (ADHD, NLD, MCDD, borderline, depression, etc.). This chapter also adds some critical notes to the current approach of autism and diagnosing adults. Some respondents ask themselves how an institute specialised in autism can be objective when diagnosing autism.

Keywords Autism • Diagnosis • Psychological tests • Psychiatry

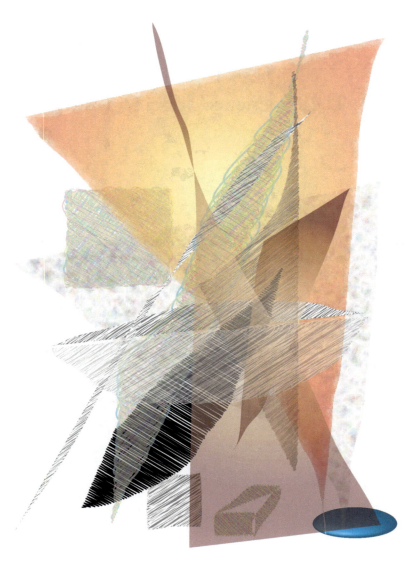

After periods of severe problems which raised a desire in them to find an explanation for what was happening, many participants decided to undergo testing for autism, often on the recommendation of a psychologist, psychiatrist, partner or family member. Some of the respondents went to a specialised facility, while others were tested during their stay in a psychiatric hospital. In addition to conventional tests for autism such as *Autism Diagnostic Observation Scale* (ADOS-2) and an anamnesis with family members, our participants also underwent cognitive tests. A few were happy with the scientific validity of the tests that were used. Others were curious about how such a test could determine autism. It was remarkable, however, how little explanation the researchers provided about why exactly they had come to the conclusion 'autism spectrum disorder' after testing our respondents.

Although various respondents offered us their diagnostic reports, we made the conscious decision not to look at them before the interviews. After all, the main focus of our project was how the participants experienced their diagnosis and the accompanying diagnostic process. The same goes for intelligence tests. Even though during the interview, some of the interviewees spontaneously shared the results of their IQ tests with us, or used expressions such as 'moderately intelligent' or 'above average intelligent' to describe their own level of understanding, we did not use this information in our analysis of the conversations. Before the interviewees described their individual test experience, we did provide them with some background information about the tests they could remember.

Many participants indicate that they went through a combination of cognitive tests and tests specifically aimed at determining autism. Besides the specific anamnesis, Marie remembers the following tests that were used for her:

IQ;	*WAIS IV*
Attention:	*Bourdon-Vos, Stroop Colour-Word test*
Memory:	*fifteen words of Rey, complex figure of Rey*
Executive functions:	*Tower of London, Wisconsin Card Sorting test*
Central coherency and ToM:	*completing dialogue, Rakitplates, How is ... feeling? Stories of Dewey, Stange stories Happé*
	Problem Solving Skills
Perception survey:	*projective material, four affects, conversation with test leader*
Questionnaires:	*SCL-90, AQ, BDI-II-NL.* [Marie]

Some participants mention autism-specific tests such as the ADOS-2 or inform us that their parents, partners or friends also underwent an anamnesis. It is striking, however, that certain participants mainly mention cognitive tests. More specifically, tests that presuppose a certain *theory* about autism (*ToM*, executive functions and central coherence).

Carl's most vivid memory from the test sessions is the assignment to draw a bicycle. He drew it from left to right, first the wheel, then the handlebar and so on, finishing at the right-hand side of the page. He was told that this deviates from what the average person would do: a normal drawing style would be to first draw both wheels, and only then to complete it with the other elements of the bicycle. Another drawing test the participants mention is the complex figure of Rey.

This drawing test is aimed at indicating whether someone has a good memory, it tests planning, organisation, problem solving, memory and perceptual–motoric functions. In the context of autism, it is also used to measure *central coherence*, the ability to see a whole instead of only the details. If the participant begins by drawing the outline, this can indicate more central coherence. If the participant initially draws a few separate details of the picture, this would indicate a deficient central coherence, as the following quotation indicates:

> *And yeah, so I started drawing, a line and a line, and a little ball there and a little line there… Especially when, after twenty minutes, they asked me a second time if I remembered the drawing, and if I would be able to draw it again, I only remembered a little line here and a little ball there. And then, afterwards, they said yeah well that's actually just a rectangle with two other triangles in it or something, and everyone sees that, and apparently I didn't see that. I thought that was really… Then I thought like yeah I really see the details and not the whole, such things really struck me about myself.* [Hannah]

This is what Sofie has to say about the test:

> *Drawing that picture, that went reasonably well. During the evaluation they said: "You start with the details, you do see the whole," I am apparently quite focused on detail.* [Sofie]

Sofie had received the results of her test only two-and-a-half weeks before the conversation with us. Eight years earlier, she also had herself tested for autism, but then the test was negative. They told her that, if she indeed had autism, it would probably only be a mild version. Sofie also remembers that she had to take other tests eight years ago. Her explanation for the fact that the test results are different now, is that back then, a lot less was known about women with autism:

> *Then, they already knew more, but I think that now, they know even more... Back then, they also didn't know that women have a different form of it than men do, right, they have figured that out more now right, maybe that's the reason too, that women are also more social, right.* [Sofie]

In addition to tests on central cohesion or focus on detail, our interviewees also mention tests that study certain *executive functions*. Executive functions are cognitive processes that make sure that we can plan ahead, and that people can solve problems purposefully. One theory about autism, which mainly explains why autists have a preference for structure and repetitive actions, states that they have a deficiency in those executive functions. Our participants also mention that they had to stack wooden beads (*Tower of London Test*) or sort cards (*Wisconsin Card Sorting Test*), they had to do tests that had them plan their shopping or find their way in a zoo. Tests which were originally solely used for the purpose of testing memory were now—in the context of autism diagnostics—apparently used to verify certain aspects we associate with autism. Baukis illustrates her personal test experience with *Fifteen words of Rey as follows*:

> *The psychologist who tested me said 15 words out loud, which I had to try to repeat afterwards. According to the test leader, I scored relatively well on that, I had an average amount of words right. He didn't mention at the beginning that he would repeat this sequence of words several times during the full course of testing, every time with the intention that I had to repeat as many words as possible. Every time I remembered about a similar amount of words, but not the same words every time. Only the last time, while I was reciting the words, I realised that I could have fabricated a story from the different words, in order to remember them more easily. That signifying and making connections apparently happens a lot later with me than with other people.* [Baukis]

For Baukis, this test took a specific course because she only started to use semantic connections to remember a list of words at a later part of the test. Further on in the conversation, she says that she considers autism a predominantly cognitive problem that can also be characterised by a recognition of, for instance, sounds and word forms as such, without automatically connecting a meaning to it. This is something neurotypical people would do more easily.

Participants remember tests that have to do with the performance of *ToM*: the ability to empathise with someone else's experience or feelings, in other words to imagine the perspective of the other. They mention the *Reading the Mind in the Eye* test, developed by Simon Baron-Cohen and his colleagues. This test assumes that the eyes are the mirrors of the soul and that, just by looking someone in the eyes, we should be able to determine what he or she feels. Autistic people supposedly score significantly lower on this test than neurotypicals. The *Strange Stories* of Francesca Happé, stories that test whether people can effectively sense someone else's perspective, are also mentioned by the participants. An example of such a strange story:

> *A burglar, who has just plundered a shop, rushes to leave the scene. While he is running, a policeman, who is doing his rounds, notices that he drops a glove. He does not know that the man is a burglar. He only wants to tell him that he dropped his glove. But when the policeman shouts at the burglar: "Hey, you! Stop!" the burglar turns around, sees the policeman and surrenders. He holds his hands high and confesses he broke in to the neighbourhood shop.*

Annelies Spek[1] tells us how this test is to be scored. The diagnostic will for instance ask: "Was the policeman surprised when he heard what the burglar said?" or: "Why did the burglar do that, when the policeman only wanted to return his gloves?" A right answer would for instance be that the burglar thinks the policeman wants to arrest him for the break-in. We could, however, think of a variety of correct answers, on the basis of which we are not able to rule out, but also not to conclude, whether the individual test candidate is able to imagine what went on inside the burglar's head. For instance:

- The force and intensity the policeman uses in his voice to stop the burglar, cause the burglar to suddenly realise there is a possibility that the policeman witnessed everything he did, even though he did not notice him before.

[1] Spek (2017).

- The burglar thinks that the policeman thinks it is suspicious that he ran so fast and he will therefore suspect that something is not right. It is therefore better for him to tell the truth.
- The burglar could have remained stoically silent, but he did not do this because he was out of breath and less alert.
- Doesn't everyone feel like the guilty party when a policeman asks you something? When there is a police car on the motorway, doesn't everyone exhibit exemplary driving behaviour all of a sudden?
- The policeman does not have to shout: "Hey, you!" If he had just shouted: "Sir!" in a friendly tone of voice, the burglar would have had a better chance to respond differently. Even if he had said: "Sir, your glove", the whole event would have been less tense and the burglar could have responded in a much calmer way.
- A policeman in uniform always means trouble.
- The burglar thought: "If I confess everything at once, I might be able to make a deal with the policeman."
- A policeman is always armed and the burglar was so afraid that something worse would happen, that he spontaneously confessed everything.
- You can always tell if someone is guilty of something, the burglar knows this. No matter how good the lie, there is always an element that gives you away.
- He who is in the right, has a strong position. The burglar was not in a strong position. This is even the case when two people argue with each other. The one who is in the right, has the strongest position. The burglar knew this and that is why he confessed to everything.
- The burglar was so nervous beforehand and was so afraid that he would get caught, that he did not realise the policeman stopped him for a different reason.

In short, we can ask ourselves what this question and the corresponding 'right answer' is supposed to prove.

In the *Handbook of Assessment and Diagnosis of Autism Spectrum Disorder*,[2] which is 478 pages long, only one chapter discusses the diagnosis of adults. This chapter contains 16 pages, including references and the disillusioning conclusion that:

[2] Iliani Magiati (2016).

> Currently, little is known about how best to assess and support individuals with ASD in adulthood. We also know little about the developmental nature of the condition beyond young or middle adulthood. Although assessment of adults with ASD should be comprehensive and lead to specific recommendations for support, provisions, and interventions, there are currently very few professionals with the required expertise and skills working with adults with ASD who can actually implement these recommendations, while adult services continue to be scarce in most countries.[3]

Apparently, according to the official literature, little is known about how to diagnose and help these adults. This is remarkable, as more and more people *are* being diagnosed in adulthood. There is, however, a table of tests available that could be used, mostly tests such as the ADOS-2 and the *Social Responsiveness Scale* (SRS), which was originally developed for children. The ADOS-2 is a standardised observation-instrument for communication, social interaction and (imaginative) play, which is used to observe whether the criteria for autism are present in a person. You can, for instance, ask children to re-enact a birthday party and observe how they interact. With older children and adults, the emphasis is more on conversations, understanding and the role of emotions.

In the stories our participants tell us, the abovementioned cognitive tests are—in addition to the standard instruments—an integral part of the diagnostic test they had undergone to determine autism. This might be a result of the assumption that normal to highly intelligent adults have often learned to conceal typical autistic behaviour, which means that the usual behavioural observation is not sufficient to come to a substantiated conclusion. This is probably why certain diagnostic centres have decided to include tests that focus on certain cognitive differences, such as memory tests or tests that determine how well people are able to read feelings, as part of the diagnostic. In this way, the practice starts distancing itself more and more from the original definition of autism as a behavioural diagnosis, as specified in the DSM. The determination of a deficient—or high functioning—memory, or deficient central coherence, executive functions or ToM can of course be very informative clinically. If these tests are part of testing for autism itself, we encounter the problem of 'tautological testing'. Research in cognitive science has established that people diagnosed with autism statistically do not score as well (or 'different') on

[3] Idem.

the complex figure of Rey (central coherence) or on the shopping test (executive functions).[4] Can we conclude from this that these tests are then automatically a fitting diagnostic tool to test autism itself?

The DSM-5 definition of autism spectrum disorder establishes that autism diagnostics are based on experience, the observation of behaviour and an assessment of the level of dysfunctioning in society. One point of criticism could be that these tests are not so much used for the results of the test itself, but rather as a way to observe behaviour during testing. Robyn describes:

> *They also did things very consciously during the tests to see how I would react, and mostly also focused on that... So basically they read between the lines, and not just did the tests and that's it. So you have to, like, do you know the test with the little balls? Yes? Well yeah, the four little balls. At a certain moment she started to very consciously click with her ballpoint, and she says, yes you can see it immediately, the line where I clicked, five seconds more reaction time. So I was very quick, average level was 9 seconds, but on the line where she did that, it was 13 seconds all of a sudden. Immediately. Or if she would turn on the lights. She said, up and away, again, skyrockets immediately.* [Robyn]

The goal of the test is to both test for executive functions and test to which extent someone is sensitive to sensory stimuli, sound in this case. It is interesting to note that in the three most-cited theories on autism (ToM, weak central coherence and weak executive functioning), the sensory sensitivities are considered to be a side issue. We can imagine that a theory on autism that localised the 'basic deficit' of autism mostly in a different sensory perception would perform different tests. It is not really problematic in itself that specific theories on autism are tested during a diagnostic process. It can be very informative to know whether someone has problems with executive functions or with understanding the perspective of the other. In that capacity, these tests can be part of a profile of strengths and weaknesses. It is still necessary, however, to integrate this in adequate counselling of the person in question.

Participants are often very happy with the scientific level of the tests that are being used. Baukis explains:

> *I'm so happy with how the test has been performed, because it initially tested how I process information. Not my background, not my story, not my motive to get*

---

[4] Kushner, E.S., Bodner, K. E., Minshew, N. J. (2009).

myself tested. That also happened, but only afterwards. The tests examined how my learning process evolves, how my memory works. What do I see in an image, what do I remember, what do I pick up from a story... Because yeah, that's what autism is essentially about for me: a different way of processing information. Period. [Baukis]

With her children, testing was done differently, with more emphasis on background and story, but that is a side issue for Baukis. Samuel also describes how happy he is that the testing was done in a serious manner. He does not agree with how the media report on these kinds of diagnostic processes, as if it were 'flick of the wrist' diagnostics, administered in a rush and without method:

It certainly helped me, in the sense that I got an image of how diagnostics was done in a serious way, and that the reports in the media are completely wrong. But it also helped me in the sense that I know that I definitely don't have schizophrenia or mental disabilities or psychopathy. It ruled out many possible explanations, even though there are people who still think that. It also helped that they made a written report, and that it could be a beginning of a road towards a better life, on the one hand to learn to understand others and also a little to protect myself. [Samuel]

Samuel describes how the tests, by determining autism, could exclude other diagnoses, and how having a written declaration has given him a foothold that enables him to keep going. Still, a few participants question how it is even possible that tests can determine whether or not someone has autism. In the fragment below, Sandra calls autism an 'exclusionary diagnosis':

Yeah and then I also underwent MMPI as well. Then they said it's to really rule out that you have no personality disorder. Now I'm sure that I don't have borderline or that I don't... Yeah but that's actually an exclusionary diagnosis, a real autism test doesn't exist, right, I think. That's more like seeing how you function memory-wise or how your intelligence functions or your verbal abilities... [Sandra]

The *Minnesota Multiphasic Personality Inventory* (MMPI) is a questionnaire that tries to map the personality of the person involved. Sandra says that this was used to exclude personality disorders such as borderline during the testing process. She argues that a real 'autism test' does not exist, but it is rather a matter of taking a look at how you function and of excluding other explanatory models. The fact that it is now, via the use of personality tests, unambiguously determined that she has no personality disorder, is very important to her. She later explains that in the past, she was often labelled dependent, attention seeking, perhaps sometimes a bit egocentric, even though she does not identify with that image at all. The correct diagnosis, she says, provides her with a correct treatment that feels good, and that she can identify with.

The idea of 'diagnoses of exclusion' also surfaces in other conversations. Tatiana, for instance, writes about *Attention Deficit Hyperactivity Disorder* (ADHD):

> *You know why they excluded ADHD for me? They gave me Ritalin and checked if it worked. Well, apparently not. It made me completely hyper. Then you apparently don't have ADHD either. I think it's all pretty vague actually, they say anthropology is pretty vague, but this is much worse. In anthropology, they at least admit that they don't know, and they also always write down why they think something, they write down their observations. Psychology and psychiatry are far more arrogant.* [Tatiana]

Tatiana, who has a degree in anthropology, has many questions about the scientific value of psychiatric diagnostics. She, for instance, describes how no one could give her a satisfying answer to the question how autism could be distinguished from *high sensitivity*:

> *Well there is also something different than autism for people who are spiritually sensitive, people who are highly sensitive or something. I asked the psychologist too, but she said: "Yes, but that's not a disorder." Well I don't simply have a disorder because you want to give me one. I think that trend is still very much in its infancy, and that psychiatry takes itself so seriously. A few years ago, the mother was still to blame, when someone was autistic, and then we blamed his surroundings, every time they think of something new. They could also say: "We don't know, but we have come up with this box for these phenomena," and if it can be biogenetically, or something, determined, well then they have to put everyone under a scan. But they don't even know themselves. Every time when I ask questions or other autists ask questions, people say: "You're being difficult, that's typically autistic, you guys are so difficult, you're so precise." Yeah but then I say: "YOU are just not thorough. Why don't you just admit what you don't know." And they so badly want to meet the requirements of biomedical science, because that's like rock-hard science, but psychiatry actually really isn't, in a way.* [Tatiana]

High Sensitive Person (HSP) is a type of personality that is mainly described by Elaine Aron. A highly sensitive person is more receptive to stimuli, which is often connected with getting tired more easily, and a desire for tranquillity and structure. In relation to these symptoms, it is unclear, for a few of our participants, how this differs from autism. Tatiana explains:

> *They can't say anything about it* [about HSP, KH] *because then you don't belong in psychiatry. And that's the inversed interpretation, right. Can you say: "I don't know enough about HSP, it could be that you have that as well, but in psychiatry you are able to acknowledge that you have these things, and maybe you have that too, but I can't say anything about that." But they don't say that.* [Tatiana]

Tatiana deconstructs her diagnosis of autism: she is diagnosed with autism and not HSP because the latter is a personality trait and not a disorder. And people already presume, instead of testing for a disorder, that she *has* a disorder, and that she therefore cannot have HSP. She also very clearly mentions her discontent with psychiatry and psychology's desire to be a biologically 'founded', and therefore exact, science. This desire unequivocally leads to the fact that people do not want to or cannot see the uncertainties in their own discipline. To Hannah, they explained that her high sensitivity was connected to her autism: "Yeah, they also say that I'm a highly sensitive person, which is also connected to that autism."

Kris also asks similar questions. Although he very much identifies with the diagnosis of autism, he thinks he has not been given enough information about how they were able to deduce that he has autism from the tests. He has asked for an explanation from the psychologist who tested him, but he has not received a univocal answer. Why does he have autism, and not high sensitivity or Obsessive Compulsive Personality Disorder (*OCPD*)? "I'm stuck with that feeling like, is that it or not really, or also highly sensitive, or also obsessive or also this and that…".

Two of the respondents have, in addition to being diagnosed with autism, also been diagnosed with a Non-verbal Learning Disorder (NLD). NLD is characterised by having trouble with spatial awareness, motor skills, social awareness and insight into cause and effect. There is often a gap between the verbal and the performal IQ, where the latter is considerably lower than the former. According to some experts, the diagnoses of NLD and autism (more specifically, the former syndrome of Asperger) are actually the same. As we already know from Chap. 3 (*Perspectives on Suffering*), Michael has both diagnoses of ASD and NLD. He explains:

> *Yeah, when I was young, it always used to be NLD. Now everything is combined: NLD is more a psychologic diagnosis, it's more neuropsychology, and ASD has more to do with psychiatry and congenital limitations in the brain. Now they combine it all.* [Michael]

During the interview, Michael indicates that he identifies more with the diagnosis of NLD than with autism, also because he thinks many people associate autism with 'not being social'. He considers himself to be rather social. He explains that being diagnosed with autism has many consequences with respect to how people around him react. This is especially problematic when it comes to expectations and the image people have of autism. As an example, he indicates that when applying for a job, a diagnosis of NLD has less of an impact than a diagnosis of autism. With autism it is as if some doors close, with NLD there is only the need to make a few amendments.

With Bluetopian, NLD was determined simultaneously with ASD:

> *I have a second disorder in comorbidity: NLD. Non-verbal Learning Disorder, which is a bad name (although conventional) and, especially in my case, more a spatial-visual disorder. So I experience ASD mostly from my NLD. On the other hand, ASD alone as a diagnosis is more of an exception. ASD almost always exists in comorbidity with other disorders, problems, psychiatric conditions etc....* [Bluetopian]

Bluetopian can often better relate to the diagnosis of NLD than to the diagnosis of autism, since this describes both his verbal strengths and his problems accurately. Here, however, we also encounter the question of demarcation between diagnoses:

> *There are different interpretations and opinions about NLD between (neuro)psychologists and psychiatrists. According to some, NLD is a different name for ASD. According to others, it is possible that NLD is a diagnosis in itself (although not recognised by the DSM-5 and therefore not recognised by the official institutions). And then there are others who frame NLD within ASD. If even the specialists don't agree, how am I supposed to find my way in it?* [Bluetopian]

Not all interviewees have positive experiences with the diagnostic tests. Marie writes that she did not think the tests were agreeable at all, she thought they were strange. This can of course also be explained by her previous experiences, as illustrated in Chap. 3 (*Perspectives on Suffering*):

> *I thought the tests were bizarre and I repeatedly asked myself how they were able to determine from those results whether someone is autistic or not. I was sometimes bothered by how the questions in the questionnaires were formulated; I thought some questions were unclear and ambiguous. I also have a tremendous aversion to questionnaires, ever since my stay in that psychiatric hospital in 2007/2008, because there I had to answer lists with hundreds of questions, but I nonetheless felt very misunderstood.* [Marie]

Vic asks himself how objective a psychiatric diagnosis can be if you are tested in a facility that is specialised in the diagnosis you are there for:

> *I ended up in that team, and they're specialised in autism for adults. In that sense I don't know, they must know a lot about it, but I think it's weird if you go for an objective diagnosis that you immediately end up in a specific team.* [Vic]

Vic wonders how people can come to the right diagnosis if they do not test the entire person, but start testing someone with a certain diagnosis in mind already.

Many interviewees received no further explanation about the reason behind the tests and, therefore, remain in the dark as to whether certain ambiguities were part of the tests or not. Carl writes about this lack of explanation:

> *For two years, six sessions of two and a half hours. And then they presented lots of things to me: tests, drawing a picture, short questionnaires, but also testing with figures, so a whole range of tests which sometimes made me wonder like yeah what's the meaning of this, and I wasn't allowed to ask those questions, and (laughs)… […] I accepted that answer at that moment and said like, I'm not going to be difficult about it, but I thought like: they will probably give me an answer afterwards. So yeah, I never got an answer.* [Carl]

Michael also thinks it is a pity that he never received further information about the tests. In the following quotation, he describes his experience with the *Reading the Mind in Eye* test, among other things:

And then I did ask after all if I could do the tests again to be able to see again like yeah, what does this say, and then it will be clear anyway. But sometimes I'll also ask: "Can I test someone myself", because I couldn't see what those tests mean or something. You've got a lot of feelings that are about the same, how can you see that in someone's face, I can tell if someone is angry or sad… but what's the difference between … (sighs) yeah sometimes not fearful, angry…,you can see that, but there is also something … I don't know, I can't directly tell but… and sometimes you can only see a small part of the eyes. And then I think, there's so many people who can't do that. That I sometimes also see like yeah, how much I scored on that little part, on those parts, because it's often only scored on autism. But sometimes I'm like, yeah, how much did I score on a specific part, and what is most difficult for me in those tests, and what's easier for me, and can I then please see those answers, but that never happened. [Michael]

The lack of clarity about the right answers to the test questions gives the diagnosis a bit of a mysterious character. In the quotation above, Michael describes that he thinks the eye test is probably also very difficult for other people.

In the following quotation, Vic reads out an excerpt of the diagnostic report and describes that he thinks that the explanation of the test is very cryptic:

"With respect to the autism specific screens, we see that the client scores above the cut-off on the AQ autism quotient. In terms of self-reported empathy, client is however still situated within the non-pathological zone…" – does that mean that I don't think I'm sick yet? – "Regarding himself, client indicates that he is still aware of the social cues around him. SRS awareness T=62, but we see nearly"– and that's what I'm on about – "but we see nearly perfect 'ceiling scores' on the sub scales that assess his capacities to interpret social signals and to communicate about them." What does that really mean, those 'ceiling scores' right? So I indicate that I'm still aware of social cues but "we see ceiling scores." So that's actually a bad thing? [Vic]

Vic thinks it is difficult to interpret the diagnostic jargon correctly. He has questions about the usage of words such as 'ceiling scores', and the difference between what was tested and what he says about himself.

Tatiana describes how the counsellors interpreted what she said differently from how she actually meant it:

During the examinations at Radboud hospital, they also asked that question [if she experiences things differently, KH]*, and I just very calmly responded.*

> *I said – and I took into account that they would interpret it differently – that there are of course things you can't see, or not everyone can see. That's quite logical, right, but what they made of it was: "MCDD, she fantasises a lot"....*
> [Tatiana]

Multiple Complex Developmental Disorder (MCCD) is also called 'children's borderline'. One of the characteristics of MCCD is confusion between fantasy and reality. Tatiana, however, interpreted the question as a factual question about invisible things. She continues:

> Tatiana: *Of course there are lots of things we don't see, it has to be, because otherwise you can't call to New Zealand on the phone, there can't be internet, there are lots of energies, and powers, and, and in life and the milky way, we can't see all that.*
> KH: *Does this make you angry?*
> Tatiana: *Well angry, no. But I really thought like don't see this diagnostically when it simply isn't. So what happened next was that I thought, you people don't even know what autism is, you really don't know what it is. It's maybe no autism at all, there's also something else, and you don't want to talk about that*

This causes Tatiana to lose her trust in the medical world, and in the possibility to scientifically determine diagnoses. Matteo also has doubts about the decisions that are being made based on diagnostics:

> *Yes for instance uhm... it says: "the processing of information seems to go in a very specific way." But afterwards they explain it as follows: "he seems to process incoming stimuli in a similar manner and to not make much distinction between main and side issues." But I* can *make a distinction between main and side issues, but – most of the times, and also in various situations – I try to always, like, follow one line, to always be myself [...].I'm not going to act differently when I see someone in the supermarket, because after that I might meet him somewhere in the woods on vacation or something. I think that's what they mean... and that I indeed have problems with that... I have problems with it, not with making the distinction between main and side issues, but with making the distinction between encountering someone in a supermarket and encountering someone in the woods, or for instance meeting that same person in a course you enrolled in or something... or if he were to enter this room now.*
> [Matteo]

He opposes the clear-cut statement that he would make too little distinction between main and side issues, but he does think that he has some difficulty with respect to context sensitivity. For Matteo, these are two separate issues. For instance, he knows cognitively that it is expected that you react differently when you see someone on holiday than when you meet them in the supermarket, but it is difficult for him to put this into practice.

Some of our respondents received no further explanation alongside their diagnoses. ASSpirin mentions, for instance, that they sent her diagnosis to her via mail. They did give her the opportunity to make a new appointment. She did not respond to this, however, because the diagnosis was clear and she did not need any additional information at that time. Els has a neurological explanation for what autism is:

The psychiatrist said: "every brain develops, but in the development of your brain there is a deficit. Every baby is born with a lot of synapses and a lot of connections. Then, that brain develops so these connections are strengthened, but also that these connections are trimmed and that channels are merged. What's left is bigger channels. With you, that's not the case, those little channels did not develop into a few big sturdy channels. So with you, all stimuli go through those many little channels while with others, more stimuli are filtered before they end up in those large pathways. With you, the filtering still has to be done by the small channels. This is why you get tired so quickly and why you are overstimulated." That tiredness is constant in my life. [Els]

It is remarkable how the explanation of what is going on in her brain can be easily translated to the problems Els experiences in daily life. The image of the hyperconnected brain is very recognisable for people who have problems with overstimulation.

In this chapter, we described how our participants experienced the tests. Many of our respondents have found that the diagnosis holds a kernel of truth, in spite of their often critical attitude towards the tests themselves. The degree of recognition that respondents experience in relation to the content of the tests is often high. The way in which themes are questioned is very much appreciated by some because of its scientific value. For others, the connection between the questioning and the conclusion is still very unclear. What all respondents have in common is an awareness that the conclusion 'autism' connects with their previous quest. In the next chapter, we will describe how being diagnosed with autism can operate as a way to cope with being different.

Bibliography

Kushner, E.S., K.E. Bodner, and N.J. Minshew. 2009. Local vs. Global Approaches to Reproducing the Rey Osterrieth Complex Figure by Children, Adolescents, and Adults with High-Functioning Autism. *Autism Research* 2 (6): 348–358. Wiley-Blackwell, December.

Magiati, Iliana. 2016. Assessment in Adulthood. In *Handbook of Assessment and Diagnosis of Autism Spectrum Disorder*, ed. Johnny L. Matson, 191–207. Autism and Child Psychopathology Series. Cham: Springer International Publishing.

Spek, Annelies. 2017. https://www.anneliesspek.nl/strange-stories/. Accessed 14 Aug 2018.

CHAPTER 5

Autism as a Way to Hold Your Own

Abstract This chapter deals with the question how one should relate to the diagnosis once it is made. Is it suddenly an explanation for all the problems you had in life? Does this mean the quest for recognition is finally over? Can everything you experience and have experienced now be explained by turning to the diagnosis? Can the diagnosis help you to think about your own identity? Many respondents recognise themselves in the diagnosis, they can relate to what it stands for. In that respect, it gives them comfort to finally 'know' what is 'wrong' with them. Some people ask which parts of their past can be explained by autism, and which parts are due to other circumstances in life. Others say that autism for them is normality, but they are aware of the fact that this normality is represented by a mere minority.

Keywords Autism • Explanation • Recognition • Diagnosis

For the participants, the diagnosis of autism spectrum disorder or Asperger's syndrome is a plausible explanation for events and experiences from the past they could not place. The diagnosis initially has a liberating effect, which forms a sharp contrast with their often problematic past. It is usually received with open arms, as a possible explanation for their being different and their unusual way of responding to people. Because of the great amount of effort the interviewees put into leading what could in general terms be considered a regular and normal life, the diagnosis seems to provide a kind of social refuge from their daily efforts. It provides as it were a kind of *inner peace*, next to the continuous anxiety people experience from being different than others and perceiving and responding differently than others do.

For many, autism is a plausible explanatory model for problems they have had throughout their lives. At times, it is coupled with a reliving of similar situations from the past that had unfolded problematically. Because the diagnosis has provided knowledge about the specific aspects of—for instance—autism, similar situations are approached with a higher alertness and more prudence, and are therefore tackled differently. Our respondents testify to profound memories which are connected to these misunderstood events, and which they have carried with them for a long time as moments of failure, or of not responding correctly or adequately. New information given by the diagnosis provides a different approach to all those misunderstood moments of the past, which enables the respondents to process the events. In this respect, the diagnosis can have an exculpating effect for those who are diagnosed: finally, there is a legitimate reason for their being 'different'.

Albert describes in the quotation below that he has had difficulty networking his entire life. A few years before the diagnosis, he joined the Rotary Club—a service club where people go to meet like-minded people and engage in philanthropy—hoping this would help him move forward a bit. This was not the case however:

> *All my life, I have felt I'm not a networker. In order to do something about this, I joined the Rotary 5 years ago. Now, all those years later, I still can't network. Ever since my diagnosis, I understand why. All my life, I have been copying people's behaviour so I wouldn't get noticed too much, and because I can't think of how I should behave in certain situations. For instance, I started crying at a funeral of someone I didn't know, only because the other people were crying.*
> [Albert]

Now that he has his diagnosis, Albert understands why he is not able to spontaneously master the art of networking. He furthermore describes that he has problems in social situations, and he only manages to remain standing by copying other people's behaviour. The diagnosis teaches him to accept his being different:

> *I no longer see myself as an alien, but just as someone with a different brain structure and a different way of thinking. I used to think that there were no limitations for me. Because of the diagnosis, I got to know my limitations much better, and also learned to respect them better (through trial and error).*
> [Albert]

As Albert indicates, this recognition goes hand in hand with his own limitations. He used to be convinced that he could handle anything as long as he tried hard enough, but now he understands that there is a *neurological* limitation to what he is able to do.

Even though some respondents received different diagnoses before they were diagnosed with autism—borderline personality disorder, OCD and so on, they consider autism to be a better explanation for who they are and the problems they encounter. Vic, for instance, provides a whole list of diagnoses he received during his several stints in psychiatric hospitals:

> *I had myself diagnosed or tested towards a diagnosis last year, because I've had so many different diagnoses throughout the years. Yeah it says here (shows diagnostic report) uh… autism spectrum disorders, OCD, schizophrenia, schizoaffective disorder, schizo-typical personality… Yeah… Two weeks ago someone said ADHD. With every different psychologist… some can already tell after five minutes…* [Vic]

Vic describes how he did not care much about the diagnoses he received from the professionals, including the autistic disorder. He did recognise himself, however, when he read the Wikipedia page about Asperger's syndrome:

> *Yeah but okay, they made me do stuff for a month or so and he eventually said the DSM-IV classification was… (reads): "autistic disorders, schizo-affective disorder of the bipolar type, dependency of several…" And then, yeah, problems within the social area a bit yeah… "Main diagnosis: autistic disorders." I was browsing a bit, I was actually looking up what schizo-affective and schizo-typical means, and then I eventually ended up with Asperger's syndrome on Wikipedia. I've not read the entire article, but what I have read is an almost identical description of my experiences and of my inner self. I mean, I can't say it any better myself than how they wrote it there. Having to master social behaviours, almost like acting, right. Now, it's much easier actually, but really as a child and as a teenager… imitation, memorising things you can say beforehand, entire conversations in my head: "If he says that, I say this, if he asks that…" or just completely shutting down and not knowing what I should do. Or being so upset that your aunt gives you a hand and your uncle a kiss (laughs) darn… Yeah what else did I read there… performing actions without having the affect… and then not knowing why, right. I didn't know anything about it, right, about that autism, so I think I thought that was a bit strange about myself.* [Vic]

Decisive points of recognition for Vic are mainly pretending to be different so you do not stand out, and not being socially spontaneous. It is also remarkable that he identifies more with the description of Asperger's syndrome—a diagnosis which, since the DSM-5, is also categorised under autism spectrum disorder—than with the description of autism.

As mainly discussed by Tatiana in Chap. 4 (*The Experience of Being Tested*), some of our participants identified with the description of HSP before they received their diagnosis. Kris, for instance, describes that his association with autism only came when the DSM-5 discussed sensory differences:

> *Well, I was mostly thinking about high sensitivity, highly sensitive person (HSP), and high sensation seeker (HSS) also for a bit. Those concepts that were originally developed by Elaine Aron, amongst others, and now further and differently developed at universities in our country. Well I was on that track for a long time, I followed a course about it and I actually started doing that again since last year, but I still felt like that may also be it, but maybe it isn't. Anyway, when I follow a course with other highly sensitive persons in a group, I also feel like, okay, I'm also regularly overstimulated and understimulated and that's definitely there. But in the DSM-5, they now actually explicitly added over and understimulation to the concept of autism, and that's what I also really identified with, by making this explicit in autism diagnostics. Now I do understand that there is a possible overlap... but for me there's still a fundamental difference between HSP/HSS and ASD...* [Kris]

Kris recognises a lot of his own experiences in the diagnosis of autism and was already convinced for a long time that these aspects characterised him, but he also seriously doubts whether *all* aspects are applicable to him.

Besides autism, Tatiana has been diagnosed with OCPD. In literature, this diagnosis is often referred to as 'comorbid with autism'. From her quotation below, we can deduce a certain perfectionism, something other participants also mention:

> *What more can I tell you about myself? I'm a perfectionist. I also got the diagnosis of obsessive compulsive personality. Things are never finished, for instance a thesis, I can never finish that, it's never enough. I can also just almost never start anything because the result will never be good enough.* [Tatiana]

In the past, Tatiana was also diagnosed with borderline personality disorder:

> *I had to tell my life story in three sessions. That took the place of the treatments and I didn't receive any medication yet. Following the report that girl – it was really a girl, 24, 25 years old – had made, the psychiatrist decided I had borderline. And he also hardly looked any further. He said: "I have good news and I have bad news. The bad news is, you've got borderline, and the good news is, you can do something about it." Well try to put up with that, right.* [Tatiana]

Tatiana did not agree with this diagnosis however, and because she had doubts about the expertise of the person who administered the test, she asked for a second opinion. This resulted in the fact that, besides a diagnosis of borderline, they also added depression and OCD to her list of diagnoses:

> *Then I went for a second opinion, and I went to the psychiatric ward of the general hospital. Then they admitted me. They already took questionnaires, also for ADHD, again the result was borderline, but also obsessive-compulsive disorder, recurring depression, dysthymia and dependency disorder. I said, oh, that's quite a lot. That they need so many is probably because you don't have one of them for the full 100%. And they thought I had ADHD, but ADHD was impossible because I was so focused as a child. That's it. And there I was, in treatment, and I thought it really was very weird.* [Tatiana]

Tatiana is very sceptic about the capacity of these tests to give a definitive diagnosis to someone, especially because in her case the different tests could indicate different diagnoses.

Many participants accept the diagnosis of autism as an adequate explanation for the differences they experience in their lives. Samuel explains:

> *I think there's a difference between experiencing differences, and being acknowledged therein. Experiencing differences is something natural for me, and it doesn't have to be negative* per se. *It's an instinctive response of people to react with aversion to what they perceive to be threatening, although I try to do that as little as possible myself. When your being different, your otherness, is acknowledged, and explanations are given for it, when it's being labelled, it feels as something positive. People take you seriously, and they make an effort to understand you. It does take some time until a plausible and workable explanation is given about the relationship with other people, an explanation which makes my life better and not just other people's lives. The explanation 'autism' comes closest to a plausible and workable explanation.* [Samuel]

For Samuel, the diagnosis is an acknowledgement of a difference that has always been there. This implies that your being different is explained and taken seriously. Thus, the diagnosis also has a social aspect, because the act of determining this being different also leads to the fact that others will make a bigger effort to try to understand this being different.

Also for BartDelam, the diagnosis was an important turning point that changed his life for the better. He had already been searching for the cause of the problems he experienced in how he functioned in daily life, for a long time. The diagnosis gave him an explanation for his problems, a tool to understand himself better and a road towards therapy:

The diagnosis was very important for me. I would even dare to say that the diagnosis has saved my life both qualitatively and quantitatively. When – before the diagnosis – I dropped out because of a depression caused by exhaustion, I told the doctor and the relaxation therapist: "something has to happen, or otherwise something will happen." I meant that things had to change drastically or I would die from a heart attack or suicide. There were indeed thoughts of suicide in order to flee from a life I couldn't handle anymore. Although I was preparing a suicide in my head, I was mostly afraid of an impulsive act. While driving, I often thought: "if I drive against that tree, all my problems will be solved" and I felt my wheel start pulling to the right. Thankfully, I was always able to correct myself. Since the diagnosis, everything has changed. For me, the diagnosis is a liberation because now I know what the underlying cause is. Although I had many reservations about the diagnosis in the beginning, it now offers an explanation for many thoughts and behaviours. It also enables me to understand others better and to reframe difficult situations. [BartDelam]

He continues with the thought that his diagnosis has been liberating:

Since the diagnosis, I can finally really be who I am. I used to think that I was myself, but that wasn't true. Unknowingly, I played a role to meet internal and external expectations. Without even noticing it myself, I wanted to pretend I was 'normal', in other words, be like most other people instead of just being myself. The concept of 'just being yourself' was completely unknown to me before the diagnosis though, because I didn't know how to picture that. [BartDelam]

A bit further on, BartDelam describes that the diagnosis provides him with a perspective on the future:

Before the diagnosis, I also couldn't even picture the concept of 'here and now'. I continuously lived in the past with my thoughts (ruminating what had happened) or in the future (preparing for everything that would come). I have also known beautiful moments, but only since the diagnosis, do I really know what living in the 'here and now' means. I don't just live in the past or in the future now, but I have learned to enjoy the things I do now. [BartDelam]

Nora explains that getting in contact with many different people with a diagnosis made her see her way of being as valuable:

When I heard several (adult) people speak about their diagnosis and their process, it struck me how many mutual differences there were. That's something I never saw before. Hearing other people's stories has helped me to understand what 'problems' are, what 'may be', what 'can be' and what 'possibilities' are. While listening to other stories, I made an important click. [Nora]

A diagnosis offers explanations and also prospects. After years of coping behaviour and the feeling of constantly having to adapt to others, a diagnosis of autism often gives people more freedom to be themselves. People are permitted to skip office parties, things that used to be major issues before. Others also seem more understanding. Nora says that the diagnosis has changed things in her relationship with her close family members: "I think it really changed a lot, that they also stopped pushing all the time, and now it sometimes even comes naturally." BartDelam describes how being diagnosed has solved many things in the relationship with his partner. Now, she better understands why he does not always immediately respond during a conflict.

Sofie has had a very traumatising life. For her, the diagnosis is an answer to the question whether her problems are due to her past or due to an innate being different:

Yeah, I actually thought um… it's going to be a loss situation like um… if I don't have it then it's because of my past, and it's a loss situation, and if I do have it, it's also a loss situation because I, I want to be able to communicate correctly. But I kind of already gave that up for a bit. I'm like, it will grow, uhm, but actually getting the diagnosis was a relief. I'm not putting myself down all the time anymore, yeah and you can't, and… I don't blame myself as much anymore. I want to keep growing, and work on it. It's not that I give up like, I'll never be able to, no I want to be able to, but uhm, if I don't succeed I no longer give myself a beating. I've actually become more relaxed… [Sofie]

After initially accepting the diagnosis, Marie still has some reservations and wonders if some things could perhaps be explained by her traumas:

> *From the tests and conversations with the test leader, it also became clear that my life has known quite a few traumatising experiences. I actually never really gave those experiences a place because I didn't consider them to be traumas, but in the end I was actually quite bothered about them… the test leader answered my question whether she doubted the diagnosis of the multidisciplinary team: "No, I have no doubts. Although I do wonder how things would look without the traumas."* [Marie]

This nicely illustrates how on the one hand, a diagnosis at a later age offers a biological, concrete explanation for problems, but on the other hand how difficult it is to regard existing problems as purely biological. Traumas and difficult periods are also an inevitable part of someone's life, in how they are processed and in how they can determine someone's identity and suffering.

After respondents receive an explanation for certain problems, they also have to relate to that explanation. Autism is, after all, defined as a disorder, but one that is quite interwoven with one's own identity. I am like this, but it is considered to be a disorder. As mentioned in Chap. 2 (*Being 'Different'*), Bas has a clear opinion on the thought-experiment "What if they would invent an autism pill":

> *It can be a thought-experiment. Say, they would invent a pill and if you take it, you stop being autistic. And I even think they're already working on something like that. But I don't think I would want to take such a pill, for the simple reason that I think this is normal. Maybe I would rather have everyone else take an autism pill, you see.* [Bas]

Bas thinks he is normal, but also says that his normality is a minority. It would be easier if everyone had autism. He also describes how the problem not always lies in a certain way of being, but in living together with people who do not share that way of being. It would be easier if society would be a bit more sensitive to people who are, for instance, more stimuli-sensitive, instead of expecting that these people adapt or get cured:

> *If we indeed shouldn't all go to the Highlands or… There are a few other, similar thought-experiments. Yes I know, pluriform society, it all sounds so nice. But would it not just be easier if there was a society with only autists, we should dare to ask ourselves these questions. And yes, instead of that pill, we could also ask ourselves: can't we simply diminish the stimuli. So not make me less bothered by it, but just that there are less stimuli. Less is more, they say.* [Bas]

The Scottish Highlands, with its vastness and tranquillity, might perhaps be a better place to live than overcrowded Belgium, says Bas. BartDelam says that the essence of autism lies in the speed of information processing. The demands of modern-day society are much too high, which has an impact on his interaction with others, he says:

> *I think I could be empathetic, I think I could be uhm yeah, assertive or something, but uhm, it's still in preparation and I have to, I really need more time for that.* [BartDelam]

Hannah elaborates on the mismatch between accepting yourself and how difficult it is to not fit in society:

> *If I could get rid of it, I would. Because I think life is much more difficult if you have it, yeah… I think life is easier without. Well, this might be very strange what I'm going to say, but perhaps I'd even rather just, instead of being a chit-chat person, just not be here at all. Because yeah, I also don't want to be a chit-chat person in the sense that I would always only talk about hollow things, but I do think that life is quite heavy to bear. I very often think, how easy would it be if I wasn't here. Not that I, that I now think like, I'm going to hurt myself or something, no, and I do think that there are a lot of nice moments in life and all, but I do think it would be a lot easier if I didn't have to go through all this.* [Hannah]

In a way, Hannah can live with her own way of being and communicating, but it is very hard for her that the world does not accept this way of being. Tatiana calls this the *McDonaldisation* of humans:

> *Yeah, I think it's quite an intolerant society. It's not only very busy and filled with obligations that people with these ways of being can't relate to. But also very intolerant, it is of course a kind of McDonaldisation of humans. It has to be like that, and everything beyond that is qualified as a disorder.* [Tatiana]

Disorder is not so much localised in the fact that you do not function correctly yourself, but rather in the fact that society makes functioning differently practically impossible.

A psychiatric diagnosis of autism, often considered a neurobiological disorder, sometimes has the effect that failure is no longer considered to be a personal failure or a consequence of not trying hard enough, but rather an inevitable consequence of having an autistic brain. Our participants recount how they became more gentle with themselves after the diagnosis. ASSpirin, for instance, explains how she considered herself to be a difficult person for years, but now has an explanation for it:

> *Up until last year, I was strongly convinced that I was a difficult person. It was also the message I got as a child at home. Now, I rewind, as it were, all choices from the perspective of this diagnosis. I actually prefer to have as little people around me as possible. From that deeper realisation, I redecorated and demarcated my life. Now I can clearly see that this has something to do with ASD. And not so much, as I thought until last year, that I was difficult or antisocial in the first place, but that there is another fundamental issue at work here.* [ASSpirin]

Baukis also describes how she scaled back her perfectionism after the diagnosis. She describes a childhood, spent in the shadows of her gifted brother, with demanding parents and where making mistakes was out of the question:

> *I really wanted to answer to that perfect model, because I thought that was a good model. My parents were both very gifted people and good students. When I got home with a 9 out of 10, I didn't get a compliment because I did well. No, they asked me where I made the mistake. Yes, mistakes, that was horrible! I did tell myself to get a 10/10 as well. A 9/10, everyone at school could say that was good, but I didn't think it was good. How does that work? How do you have to deal with that? I never learned. How can you deal with wanting to be perfect and not being perfect, how, how?* [Baukis]

Throughout her life, Baukis had to face several failures and feelings of not succeeding. She used to connect this to the eating disorder she had, but realised that a few aspects of how she (dys)functioned in daily life date from after her eating disorder:

> *The explanations for the difficult course my life had taken [polio, eating disorder, difficult marriage, difficult divorce, KH] always covered part of the problem, but never all of it. I never had problems sensing my children, all three of them have a diagnosis of ASD. With my children, I really, without any problems, sensed the limits: when you can keep pushing, and when you'd better stop. I thought I recognised that from my experiences with being 'different', being weaker than many peers. That, I experienced during my eating disorder. Strangely enough, it never occurred to me that I could also have ASD. Until I saw similarities in the behaviours of my children with my own behaviours after my eating disorder.* [Baukis]

Els also speaks about the time before and the time after diagnosis. Before she knew she had autism, she had a big fear of failure, but now, after the diagnosis, she dares to do a lot more without fear. She says that because of the diagnosis, she is going through many changes:

> *I think I will always keep separating my life in before and after the diagnosis. I think that I may not have changed much, but that I'm still changing. Before the diagnosis, I used to be very insecure, clearly intelligent, but I didn't want to know it myself. I was always afraid of what people might think of me when I did something. As a child, I was terribly shy but I did blossom, especially when I started my studies. But insecurity and anxiety have always been there. I first have to prove myself extremely well before I'm sure it's okay.* [Els]

BartDelam also describes how he became less strict with himself after the diagnosis:

> *Sometimes consciously, but mostly unconsciously, I tried to meet the norms, whatever they may be. Expectations from the outside were unconsciously internalised, as if they came from within myself. I did set high demands for myself to meet the norms. This made me to go to extremes all the time, that I had to persevere and in doing so, I overstepped my own boundaries. Now, after the diagnosis, I no longer feel the need to meet the norm and to fit in. I have been able to put this aside for the greater part, because I realise that that's actually not possible and that I'm different than the others. I still try to do my best, but I no longer desperately want to be the same as others. Now, they just have to 'take me or leave me'.* [BartDelam]

Conforming to the norm is no longer necessary, it is simply no longer possible after the diagnosis. Robyn, who studied physics, explains how the diagnosis has given her insight into the fact that she has to translate her experiences to those of others. She used to have many moments where communicating with her friends and family was difficult, but now she knows why that is: she thinks differently and has to find a way to translate two very different ways of thinking, referring, analysing and making connections, into each other:

> *Yeah, yeah, it feels a bit like you have two reference systems, and coming from physics, you need a metric to be able to do the translation from here to there, and now I realise. Like ah, I just need that metric. I used to always think like but why can't I, why doesn't it work for me. But now I realise, I think differently, I have different parameters I work with. And that makes it much easier. Now it's*

just like ah yeah, okay, I just have to find a metric in order to be able to communicate with that other world, and then it does work. [Robyn]

Some of the participants explain that they had a kind of 'holiday feeling' in the period immediately following their diagnosis. Still, ASSpirin and Albert also remember a feeling of mourning. ASSpirin explains how, for 52 years of her life, she thought she was difficult and antisocial. In those 52 years, she did not have a diagnosis of autism as a legitimate explanation for her behaviour, which could have made her life easier. Albert refers to the classic stages of mourning by Kübler-Ross[1]: things are as they are and not differently, and he can only accept that now. Hannah, too, recounts a feeling of loss:

Life has never been easy for me, but I have always had the feeling that it got better, from kindergarten to elementary school, to middle school, to higher education. Starting to work was more difficult. But I have always had the feeling, gradually my life will get better and, if I just try hard enough, I'll get there. You see, it's getting better and better. And with that diagnosis, I actually got the confirmation that I'll never make it. I will never be able to do what someone else does. When I see my sister-in-law, how she organises her household and then with children and this and that, and then I think, yeah, I simply can't do that. I actually can't handle that lifestyle, that bustle of our current society. And that has to do with the fact that there are so many other things that ask a lot of energy from me, and I think that's difficult to accept. Because I now have the confirmation that I'm different than others and that I'll not be able to do those things. Because I have to accept that. While I always used to think, if I just try hard enough, I'll make it. [Hannah]

The diagnosis excludes a few possibilities people thought they did have before. This can be difficult to accept. This is also the reason why Nora initially resisted the possibility to get tested:

I wasn't open to the tests. On the one hand, I very much had the feeling that the diagnosis was already made even before I started with the tests. On the other hand, when the diagnosis was communicated to me, there was little room for interpretation, for reflecting on what a label or diagnosis could mean. Apart from that, I was also very angry because it took something away from me: for more than 15 years, I had very consciously tried as hard as I could to be like my

---

[1] Elizabeth Kübler-Ross calls these stadia: denial, anger, bargaining, depression and acceptance.

brother and sister; to be social, to be a good sister, to be a good child, and so on. I very strongly felt that when someone gave me a label, it also took the courage away from me in the sense that they said: "you can try as hard as you want, you will never be like your brother or sister, because there's something 'wrong' with you." In that message, I didn't only hear that I wasn't 'equal to' and as 'worthy as', but also that all my efforts had been for nothing and that it would be better for me to stop wanting and trying lots of things. [Nora]

Autism is often described as a neurological disorder you have from the day you are born, and thus your entire life. Our participants explain how this knowledge about themselves has made them more gentle, less strict with themselves, and helped them to better appreciate their own problems. This does not mean, however, that they fatalistically accept their own shortcomings. The diagnosis is in most cases a starting point from which people can better understand *and* surpass their own shortcomings. Carl explains that the diagnosis has provided him with the insight that enables him to take a step back and realise that he sometimes pushes too hard in conversations:

By doing that myself, by keeping that in mind, by staying alert during conversations or when I recount something, and being aware of 'this could be a moment when I start pushing'. Before my diagnosis, I would have thought that no one listened to me, no one hears me and this is very important, what I've got to say. Now I can take a step back and say: "Oh, it could be that someone else sees it differently." [Carl]

Due to the diagnosis, you can see how someone else could perhaps perceive you, and you can consequently appreciate the perspective of the other. BartDelam describes how the diagnosis made him understand that his own perspective might perhaps not always be the right one:

Before the diagnosis, I had a fundamental distrust in people. I also had quite some prejudices about others, based on my own anxieties. Since the diagnosis, I know that this is because I don't understand people very well. Since then, I try to go introspectively, instead of always thinking the other is the cause of the problems. Now, I better understand how my way of thinking has influenced my negative image of others, and I can counter this more quickly from a different perspective. [BartDelam]

It remains a difficult exercise, however, to see in which areas you can still improve or surpass yourself, and where you cannot:

You know Kristien, my life was all about surviving and struggling. Staying upright and continuing. With willpower and setting goals. Now, I'm really at a turning point or turning period, the nest is empty, the diagnosis is there, searching for new goals. Being gentle lies in accepting the good bits and the bits that are not so good, looking for strengths and living them, and living the things that are not so strong. Searching for 'where can I move up, and where not?' [ASSpirin]

A strong example of the potential of 'surpassing oneself' comes from BartDelam. He has written down a few helping thoughts, which help him to continue when he is about to get stuck. In the quote below, he describes how the insight in the thought process of someone with autism—and thus in his own thought process—teaches him to tackle difficult situations:

During my depression, I followed relaxation therapy. During that therapy, I had to look for a word or a term that I could use to relax. I chose 'let go'. Everything felt like lead on my shoulders and I just wanted so badly to learn to let go. This method worked so well for me, that I tried the same with different words and phrases for different situations. And thus a whole list of 'helping thoughts' developed. Helping thoughts are words or short sentences that help me to skip the usual, extensive and inefficient stream of thoughts, in order to come to a better decision or result. The thought process of someone with autism is often compared to a roadmap. With neurotypical people, the thought process goes via the motorways, which helps people to quickly go from A to B. With autistic people, thoughts go via the little roads, including a lot of detours. I still can't use the motorways (because of my autism), but with the helping thoughts (signposts), at least I no longer take major detours. For my perfectionism, I for instance use the helping thought '80/20'. This refers to the Pareto principle, which states that with 20% effort you already reach 80% of the result. In order to reach perfection, you therefore still need 80% of the total effort. That helping thought reminds me of the fact that at a certain point, I'm allowed to say that the result is good, that I can leave it like that and that it's unreasonable to strive for perfection. When I now write an email for instance, I don't have to reread it four times in order to take out all the spelling and language mistakes. Rereading the email once is usually sufficiently satisfying already. [BartDelam]

BartDelam put these 'helping thoughts' on different slides, and he has given us permission to publish one of these slides in this book.[2] He has also given us an extensive interpretation of how the helping thoughts work, as well as a description of some of these thoughts.

---

[2] See Appendix (The Helping Thoughts of BartDelam).

Our respondents describe how being diagnosed with autism provides them with an explanation for the problems they have experienced throughout their lives. Autism is a description of how they function in daily life, with which they can relate to the other and which they more or less accept. In a qualitative study by Bargiela and colleagues, we find a description of 14 women—many of them had already received a diagnosis, for instance a personality disorder, in the past—who were diagnosed with autism when they were adults. The researchers ascribe this to the fact that women are better able to hide their autism. They also describe that their participants often welcome their diagnosis, since the diagnosis enables them to give their problems a name and to talk about them. This is similar to what our participants describe.[3]

The diagnosis of autism often suggests—or is regularly interpreted as such—that someone with that diagnosis would not be able to logically think about him or herself. And that everything that they go through 'happens' to them and that they are a victim to their circumstances. In the next chapter, we will demonstrate that this is far more complex and that there is not a single correct way of thinking. The interviews demonstrate, after all, that the participants reflect on themselves extensively, and that they for the most part do not coincide with how they (dys)function.

Bibliography

Bargiela, S., R. Steward, and W. Mandy. 2016. The Experiences of Late-Diagnosed Women with Autism Spectrum Conditions: An Investigation of the Femail Autism Phenotype. *Journal of Autism and Developmental Disorders* 46 (10): 3281–3294.

---

[3] Bargiela, Steward and Mandy (2016).

CHAPTER 6

The (In)ability to Self-Reflect

Abstract The popular assumption that autistics are supposedly unable to reflect on themselves is clearly refuted by this book and the testimonies of the respondents. This chapter focuses on this (in)ability to self-reflect and shows us how the respondents reflect on themselves, and how varied and subtle these reflections are. Many of these reflections deal with our interviewees' interaction with others, they show us in-depth analyses of situations and an awareness of their own limitations and how they consciously deal with this. This chapter also addresses the question of language and means of expressing oneself and how current reality—also of psychologists and psychiatrists—is dominated by conventional truths on communication.

Keywords Autism • Self-consciousness • Reflectivity • Identity • Language

"Who are you?" is not an easy question to answer. Generally, people answer this question from the perspective of what they do, wherein they exist, and in which context they operate. Our respondents also seem to find this question difficult, but at the same time their answers are so broad and different that this can at least be called remarkable.

In *Autism. Explaining the Enigma,* Uta Frith tries to find a theory to explain autism. This explanatory model states that autistic people have a deficient self-awareness. With this theory, she wants to explain deficits in central coherence, executive functions and a deficit in ToM, as well as the fact that autists often have deviant sensory experiences. She makes a distinction between being aware of experiences on the one hand, and the experiences themselves on the other hand. Someone with autism who is insensitive to pain, supposedly feels this pain, but he is not aware of it. Conversely, oversensitivity to—for instance—sound is then not explained by the fact that people perceive a sound louder than it actually is, but because what people hear is interpreted incorrectly. These conclusions have caused Frith and Happé to take autobiographies of autistic people with a pinch of salt. The truth(fulness) of their stories should be double checked with the close circle of friends and acquaintances and/or with their family members.[1] This generated a lot of response. Linda Shriber, for instance, states that the degree of self-insight of autistic people—despite the fact that their personality develops differently—does not differ from the degree of self-insight of neurotypically developed people.[2] Victoria McGreer also argues that people, by writing their autobiographies, actually want to accomplish that others understand them.[3] They want to be respected as a person. They are not only aware of their own experiences, but also of the fact that the experiences of others are different.

In this book, we assume that autistic people can very meaningfully recount their own experiences. It strikes us that they think extensively and profoundly about what it actually means to be yourself. Some of the interviewees explicitly explain how they search for who they really are. Moreover, we wonder whether anyone can really be a self-reflective person, whilst thinking about the concept of a unified self. Can you reflect on yourself at all without verifying this with the other? The philosopher Wilhelm Dilthey states, for instance, that you cannot know yourself if you are not confronted with the other.[4] Our interviewees, too, discovered they were different by being confronted with the other, and along the way created—through conflicts and confrontations with the other—an image of what it means to be different. Carl describes how you need someone else in order to be able to think of yourself:

> *I think I just have to recognise, or perhaps generalise, that it is very difficult as a person, to reflect on yourself. That you simply need someone else for that. So that also means you show yourself with your entire heart and soul. I often noticed that during an encounter, I have already thought of several different scenarios, and have already made myself suspicious even before that other even thought something about me at all.* [Carl]

Several people point out that it is difficult for them to talk about themselves, or to answer open questions. Although some of the participants were happy to see the questions beforehand, practically no one found it problematic to speak about their own experiences. In the following

---
[1] Frith and Happé (1999).
[2] Schriber, Robins and Solomon (2014).
[3] McGeer (2004).
[4] Dilthey (1990).

quotation, Bluetopian manages to describe himself in a few fitting terms, after first hesitating and even conquering an aversion to answering open questions about himself:

> *It's very hard for me to speak about myself in the first person. Not just because I think it's hard to use the first person, but because it's difficult for me to talk about myself. I have a very strong tendency to start talking more generally, theoretically, pretty early on in the conversation. It happens more with autists, that they don't really like to talk about themselves. In all honesty, I also have to overcome a certain resistance in order to answer this question. Spontaneously, I think: why do I have to explain who I am? People will notice who I am. I also don't really know who I am. That's exactly what the problem is. I just don't like to talk about myself. I could describe myself as conscientious, a moralist (are things good or evil, equal opportunities, human rights, animal rights, justice…), a perfectionist, someone who always thinks (a thinker), someone who continuously analyses situations and others.* [Bluetopian]

Robyn describes her thought process, when she receives an open question, as follows:

> *No, no, no, no, but I'm still thinking, because now you ask, you pose the question too generally for me. So what happens now in my head is 'difficult situation, difficult situation', and then I go… and you say: "lately", in my head it goes like: "lately, okay, that's about a year, okay, what have been the difficult situations this year", okay, then I have to think back, "a year…" And then I start to scan everything, now… So it's going to take a lot of time when you ask me a question like that.* [Robyn]

Robyn states that the question "please tell us about a difficult situation you were involved in" is too open for her. When that happens, her mind starts to spontaneously envision all possible implications of the question.

What struck us during the conversations is that many of the participants explicitly and frequently think about their own thought processes, about the meaning of concepts, about what it means to have certain feelings. In the next chapter (*To Challenge or to Accept*), Sofie—who has a 28-year-old son—explains to us how she thinks about what it really means to care for someone:

> *Yes, I regularly think about what it means to care for someone. For instance, my son got a haircut. I wasn't present when that happened, he always had long*

hair, and then I think like – it may be silly right, it's even the first time I ever said this – will I still care for him after that? Well, and then I noticed now, caring doesn't depend on hair, but for me it's immediately an issue, will I still care for him, will I recognise him… [Sofie]

This quotation illustrates that Sofie is actively learning from experiences and that certain incorrect assumptions, for instance, that caring for someone would be determined by how someone looks can also be corrected.

People also think about what it means to be a person. In the next quotation, Carl describes his feeling that some days, he is more present than other days. He also speaks about the fact that when he is very conscious about not making mistakes, it is quite possible that at that exact moment, mistakes happen. Carl has, however, also experienced that when he really concentrates, good things can be achieved as well. The issue for Carl is that he is not under the impression that he can consciously influence this:

Well, that's daily business for me. You could say, every day I have to make sure that I'm present. But you're not always consciously thinking about that. So, it can happen because of an agreement, it can happen because of something someone says to me which I experience as a confrontation… Well, you could perhaps compare it to participating in traffic, when you're not focused on one specific thing, it works. But if you keep focusing on something specific whilst driving, you will almost definitely cause an accident. And thus I sometimes have that experience, that when I'm really concentrating on something, I completely miss the point. And yet, you can't put it that strongly, because there are also moments when I'm focused on something, and someone else will say: "this is genius", you see. But I don't really, uhm, specifically have that distance, these are all coincidences to me. [Carl]

A lot of our participants have created autobiographical writings, which is of course very interesting. Samuel, for instance, has a popular blog. BartDelam wrote down his experiences with tests and his own being different in a ring binder with documents. Baukis explains how she kept a diary ever since she was ten, she is now 60 and the diaries fill the space below her bed. ASSpirin participates in testimonies about autism. Robyn is writing a book, and Els is also writing a book in the context of a literary creation course:

I'm also following a course in literary creation, next year I want to graduate with a book. And it was initially about the bullying at work I had to deal with.

> I wasn't the only one who was bullied, it happens more often within the government. I talked to someone from HR and he suggested that I would be of help to many people if I wrote a book about that. But now I also connect that bullying to my autism, I was an easy target because of my vulnerability. [Els]

Els started writing this book before being diagnosed with autism, and initially wanted to write it about the bullying she experienced at work. Now, having the diagnosis has brought her so much clarity that this will probably become an important subject of her book.

Samuel writes about why autistic people feel such a need to share their experiences in a book:

> I think that writing is a way of taking something out of your head – a bit like software programs do with junk files – also a bit of going public, a bit of like developing a custom-made social prothesis and also a bit of making concrete what you have done. [Samuel]

The idea of writing as social prothesis is elaborated on by Leni van Goidsenhoven and Anneleen Masschelein, in the context of their article on an autobiographical blog about autism. They describe how writing can help you build a bridge with the outside world.[5] In other articles, van Goidsenhoven explains that writing an autobiography is a way to escape the restraints of a diagnostic label.[6] By writing about yourself and sharing your experiences with your diagnosis with others, you can work with the limitations and boundaries of the category, and integrate that category with other labels or identities (brother, author, wife...).[7]

Robyn describes, in a very gripping way, that it is very hard for her to understand feelings:

> That, that we can't understand how your world is, your emotional world. And that feelings are very incomprehensible for us anyway. That we can't fathom that. Feelings are like animals in the zoo: you people can say "that's a zebra", and describe it. For us, emotions are something like, yeah, that's an animal, but we don't really see what you see. We see animals... And you can say: "yeah but that's fear and that's sorrow and that's panic", but for me it's all exactly the same. If I then feel fear, my psychologist says: "you look afraid." And then I think, do I look afraid? So, is this fear? Yeah... [Robyn]

---

[5] Masschelein and Van Goidsenhoven. *Posting Autism*. (2016a).
[6] Van Goidsenhoven (2017).
[7] Masschelein and Van Goidsenhoven. *Donna Williams' Triumph*. (2016b).

The feeling Robyn describes here, corresponds with what psychologists call *alexithymia*: not being able to determine feelings. She does give a very accurate description of what that means to her. Through reflecting on the problems she has with feelings, Robyn reaches a very clear insight about what it means to have these problems.

In the video *In My Language* (2007) Amanda Baggs strikingly depicts that linguistic communication is not the only way one can relate to reality.[8] Baggs is diagnosed with 'low functioning autism' because she does not use oral language. With this clip, she questions what it means to be low functioning. She shows her own language: a more direct way to handle reality, by humming and feeling. Her way of communicating is not inferior, but is different. It is a frequently heard expression that humans are linguistic beings. Usually, we automatically think about the spoken word. But why would other ways of expressing not be just as good? A few participants indicated that they (also) feel comfortable with other ways of expressing themselves. Nora explains that she perceives many things visually, and that she spoke to someone else diagnosed with autism, using little cards with names written on them:

> *He actually wanted to explain 'relations' to me; relations between him and me, and more specifically how he felt emotionally towards me. He did that with the help of self-made cards. On each card, there was an emotion written down. There were about 9 cards on the table in a specific constellation which portrayed how he thought about a 'friendship'. Then he started to rearrange the cards to explain how everything evolved between him and me. It was his way of saying to me that he had fallen in love and that it became difficult to keep that other – friendly – relationship. The feeling, and more importantly, the extreme clarity of what was being said whilst rearranging – the different moves that were possible – from and between these cards, I will never forget that. Rarely have changes, mutual relations and relationships been communicated so precisely and so clearly that they started to make sense and mean something.* [Nora]

Nora experiences communicating with each other by way of little cards and images to be much more expressive than the spoken word. Nora very much likes to dance, and even considered becoming a professional dancer, until she fell into a depression after her studies. She also explains that she does not like to be in the spotlight—an inherent problem to be able to

---

[8] https://www.youtube.com/watch?v=JnylM1h2jc

practise this profession. Dancing—without pressure—is still an important way to express herself however. Nora calls this "one of the most blissful moments."

Bas has also experienced that therapists do not completely consider different ways of expressing to be as valuable as communicating through language. Bas is a musician, he has been making music ever since he was a child and he only plays his own creations. He also ran a music store for a while. For him, music is a natural form of expression. Although he expected that he would be diagnosed with autism, he has problems with the diagnostic report:

> *I didn't have problems with the fact that the autism was confirmed. I was actually happy with that, because it corresponded with my expectations. If they would have said: "No, you don't have autism, but you do have schizophrenia", that would have been very difficult for me of course. But I was very critical of the report they wrote. There were things in it of which I thought, how is it even possible that you write this when you have examined me for a year. After everything I told them, the report for instance said: "the patient – you're a patient all of a sudden as well – has very limited inner experiences." So you read that, and I also went back and said: "I don't mind if you say something like: patient finds it very hard to express his inner experiences in Dutch." I don't mind that at all, but the reality is exactly that these inner experiences are actually so rich that you can't just simply start explaining it in Dutch. Music is for instance actually also a language, a language wherein I can let these experiences out much more easily. A language which is even formed by doing it, because in a spoken language you can still think, first the message, and then you use the language to transfer that message. But with music, the medium is the message itself. The meaning comes into being, only by doing it.* [Bas]

During the diagnostic process, Bas had asked if he could express his feelings through music instead of language. They refused. For the diagnostic, someone's inability to express their inner experiences in language is the proof of a lack of these experiences. For Bas, however, spoken language is insufficient to express his experiences. In the last sentence of the quotation above, Bas furthermore questions if inner experiences can exist at all, separately from its communication.

Our participants specifically choose not to ignore the question of who they are. Moreover, this question explicitly confronts them with everything they have already experienced throughout their lives. With this in mind, we have to conclude, along with our respondents, that the assumption that people with a diagnosis would be unable to think about themselves, is incorrect. It is true, however, that our interviewees indicate that there are different forms of meaningful communication and that for them a discomfort with spoken language does not automatically imply that people are unable to communicate. Good examples hereof are the drawings in this book that precede each chapter. What is expressed in these drawings is of equal importance as the written text; reading or understanding what it means, however, cannot be done in a literal way. In these unconventional ways of communicating, 'the other' has to make an extra effort to understand the communicator, whereas usually, it is exactly the other way around for people with a diagnosis. In the next chapter, we will focus specifically on the image of autism that is established in society at large, and how our respondents are confronted with that image and the fact that they, as a person, never completely coincide with their diagnosis.

Bibliography

Dilthey, Wilhelm. 1990. Ideen Über Eine Beschreibende Und Zergliedernde Psychologie (1894). In: *Die Geistige Welt*, 139–240. Gesammelte Schriften, Vol. 5. Vandenhoeck & Ruprecht.

Frith, U., and F. Happé. 1999. Theory of Mind and Self-Consciousness: What Is It Like to Be Autistic? *Mind and Language* 14 (1): 1–22. Wiley.

Masschelein, Anneleen, and Leni Van Goidsenhoven. 2016a. Posting Autism. Online Self-Representation Strategies in Tistje, a Flemish Blog on 'Living on the Spectrum From the Front Row'. In *Disability and Social Media: Global Perspectives*, ed. M. Kent and K. Ellis. London & New York: Ashgate.

———. 2016b. Donna Williams's 'Triumph': Looking for 'the Place in the Middle' at Jessica Kingsley Publishers. *Life Writing* 13 (2): 1–23. Taylor & Francis.

McGeer, Victoria. 2004. Autistic Self-Awareness: Comment. *Philosophy, Psychiatry, and Psychology. Special Issue* 11 (3): 235–251. Johns Hopkins University Press.

Schriber, Roberta A., Richard W. Robins, and Marjorie Solomon. 2014. Personality and Self-Insight in Individuals with Autism Spectrum Disorder. *Journal of Personality and Social Psychology* 106 (1): 112–130. American Psychological Association.

Van Goidsenhoven, Leni. 2017. How to Think About 'Autie-Biographies'? Life Writing Genres and Strategies from an Autistic Perspective. *Language, Literature and Culture* 64 (2): 1–17.

CHAPTER 7

To Challenge or to Accept

Abstract Our participants express an inherent ambiguity with respect to the diagnosis of autism. On the one hand, it offers an explanation and a possible way out of the existing problems. On the other hand, it is impossible to completely coincide with a phenomenon that is as heterogeneous as autism. The danger exists that you will regard yourself solely as defined by the diagnostic label. Is it true that 'accepting' the diagnosis means that you accept a disorder which, according to certain interpretations, is a life sentence? The distinction that originates in formulating and discovering 'being different' is therefore of vital importance, more than 'being autist'.

Keywords Autism • Diagnosis • Label • Acceptance • Challenges

Although the diagnosis initially comes as a relief, people diagnosed with autism will eventually start looking for ways to relate to this diagnosis. After all, the concept of autism carries many connotations which are too numerous and diverse to be applicable to a single person. In an analysis of conversations with parents of children with a diagnosis, Jessica Lester elaborates on how broad the concept of autism is, and that people to a certain extent also ascribe their own meaning to it:

> *Parents, practitioners and society, then, by orienting to autism as having shifting meanings, might avoid constructing fixed and stable identities for and with those with whom they work and interact, inviting parents and individuals with autism labels themselves to offer accounts that function to shape and reshape their social realities.*[1]

Jennifer Singh also describes—on the basis of an interview study—how much 'work' parents have to do after the diagnosis in order to internalise

[1] Lester (2012).

the diagnosis of their child.[2] This shows us that autism is not at all conclusive as an explanation in itself: people more or less recognise their child in certain characteristics and connotations. In this chapter, we assess to what extent this also applies to adults. Do they also have to internalise the diagnosis?

After the diagnosis, many of the interviewees read books and searched for information about autism. Els, for instance, explains that books and lectures are very useful to her. Sofie is also still reading up on autism. Being diagnosed with autism implies that there is a disorder, and that the diagnosed are entitled to adjustments at work and/or sick leave. Vic explains that he qualifies as disabled, but asks himself *why* he is disabled:

> *I'm disabled, but… I do have the limitations, right. For instance, what bothers me most, apart from the depressive moods, is agoraphobia. I can't freely move like any other person. But apart from that I really feel… I wonder why I'm disabled. Especially when I'm not challenged… I think I used to be confronted with difficult situations more often, or ran into things which caused me to show symptoms. But now I have arranged my life in such a way that that hardly ever happens. Unless it takes me by surprise. For instance, when someone calls me and says: "come, let's get in the car and drive there because there's a party going on." Then I'm like, no way right.* [Vic]

Vic says he only feels disabled in certain situations. Now that he has a peaceful life with a certain structure, and he no longer has to go outside, he does not feel bad. The aspect of disability only comes to the fore when unforeseen circumstances invade his life.

An existing cliché is that autistic people are automatically good at ICT and should therefore simply find a job in the computer industry. Vic, and also Hannah, disprove this. Vic says he is not good with computers at all, and Hannah thinks the omnipresence of screens in society is disturbing. It is remarkable that a large number of participants have jobs that one would not initially associate with autism. One participant is a doctor, another previously owned a catering business at the coast, and there is even a mystery shopper amongst them. Several participants are teachers. Baukis explains:

> *At first, teaching would appear contradictory for someone with autism. But it actually isn't, because when you teach, you're in charge, you've got predictability.*

---

[2] Singh (2016).

> Following a course, or sitting in a classroom where everyone has to listen and be silent, fine. But with group work, when I don't know what's going to happen, terrible. I nearly die. [Baukis]

Teaching is, according to Baukis, on the one hand contradictory for someone with autism, perhaps because it is stressful and it instantly brings the person into contact with a group that consists of several people. On the other hand, the love for teaching can be very well explained by the fact that the teacher has the power to impose his own structure.

Bas expresses his desire to keep his uniqueness as follows:

> I think many other people could be more easily identified than me, with only a few labels, and I really think that it's more difficult for me to answer that question,[3] just because I'm not as uncomplicated as that. [Bas]

Nora has problems with how the diagnostic study was performed on her sister, because her sister very much identified with her label, and also started to re-interpret her past solely from the perspective of the diagnosis:

> Although I'm very different from my sister character-wise, I know that this does not automatically mean that she can't get the diagnosis of autism spectrum disorder. Well, she was diagnosed with it, very recently. She became very unstable because of the diagnosis, she started to re-interpret her entire past and completely lost her identity. In the end, a second opinion completely refuted the first and there was no mention of autism, but of something completely different which also required a completely different approach. On top of that, she really needed therapy to help her deal with stuff. It wasn't something of a 'lasting nature', but an 'occasional problem', irrespective of how long it drags on. For me, this was a very important event in the sense that I have a lot of questions about diagnostic processes. The diagnosis has helped me, and I'm not against diagnoses, but at the same time I have a lot of questions about certain processes, with its transparency, the scientific authority and the conclusions that are sometimes too easily made. [Nora]

The explanatory value given to a diagnosis of autism runs the risk of interpreting every aspect of your personality and actions according to that 'truth'. It can, however, also just be an explanation that offers some peace. Carl explains how difficult it is to find the right balance between the two:

---

[3] "Please tell us something about yourself. How would you describe yourself?"

> *I mean, imagine you say like yeah if that happens I will react like this. First of all, that's simply not true, because every event is different. But you could say, perhaps there is a tendency to react that way, that may be possible. That can help me orientate, to say like, I must be careful of that. Okay. But, if I do that too strongly, I become an oddball, so you can't continue with that either. You see? So the aspect of having a diagnosis, and being considered strange, no one wants that, I think. But the aspect of, okay, I know that I have to be wary of certain things, but also not too strongly... yeah that can help sometimes...* [Carl]

Rather than explaining his actions in deterministic terms, Carl describes the diagnosis as a way to orientate yourself, to become aware of potential challenges that could occur.

The idea of autism is associated with a couple of traits that participants usually do not identify with. A frequently heard cliché about autistic people is that they are not social or supposedly lack empathy. In the following quotation, Sandra challenges this assumption. She explains that she feels that not meeting the social norm entails that people automatically think you are simply not social. Sandra would explain it differently:

> *I'm described as someone who's not social. But for me, being social has got something to do with being open to other people, and letting other people be who they are and helping them. That's being social for me, that you care if someone has a problem or something, that's being social. But for many people, I think, being social is going somewhere together, sharing something together, having the same opinion together, having many people around you and throwing lots of parties, these kinds of things. For me, that has nothing to do with being social.* [Sandra]

For Sandra, being social clearly does not mean *looking for social contacts*, but rather letting people be who they are, as she indicates at several moments during the conversation. In that respect, she even considers herself to be more social than other people. Michael, too, who has a side job as a mystery shopper, contests the assumption that autistic people could never be social, that they have no friends or have problems addressing other people:

> *But I dare to address people perfectly, I mean I also go to these shops, I also speak to these people, I also go to BMW for a sales talk. I totally don't mind. I also have friends, so – okay... I also like working on my computer but I'm not like only sitting behind a computer and never speaking to people or something. I also use Facebook, right, so... Yeah okay there are also people with ASD who don't use that or something...* [Michael]

One of the most well-known explanations for the social problems autistic people experience is that they have a deficient ToM. Autistic people supposedly have problems understanding the other, or at least, this is generally assumed. Various respondents indicate, however, that understanding another person *is* possible, but that it sometimes just does not happen naturally. It can take more time and it sometimes even requires a translation in order to enable both parties to understand the different thinking patterns. The testimonies of the interviewees about their continuing search in the world around them, can lead to a more gentle point of view than, for instance, Simon Baron-Cohen has in his book *Mindblindness*. He affirms the observed inability of autistic people to imagine what goes on in someone else's mind. Baron-Cohen bases this on the distinction between empathising and systematising, wherein his research data indicate that the ability to systematise is overdeveloped in people with a diagnosis of autism.[4] Some of our participants, however, are clearly very occupied with trying to figure out what the other person thinks and feels. Hence, it would be interesting to further examine to what extent it may—for some people with a diagnosis of autism—not be a matter of inability, but rather a matter of a differently managed ability to know what goes on in someone else's mind.

Other explanatory models of autism are also challenged. Bas, for instance, states that the focus on detail (*weak central coherence theory*) is a matter of perspective. In the next quotation, he refers to his experience that others, after visiting a concert, do not seem to have noticed certain issues:

> And yeah, in NT [neurotypical, KH] *language, people say that 'the autist is focused on detail'. For instance, that music, there, that note played in that way. And then I wonder: what's detail oriented about that? Isn't it just simply the heart of the matter? I should say exactly the opposite: if there were a minority of neurotypicals, what's typical about neurotypicals? That they focus on details, on the bar of a concert hall for instance. So I could actually say the same about them.* [Bas]

Bas gives an example of the concept of context blindness, which is often associated with autism, and says that it is a matter of perspective. He has problems with the fact that when he goes to the pharmacist, they ask him

---

[4] Baron-Cohen (1997).

if everything is okay. This question is absurd. No one is—so he says—ever completely okay. Furthermore, the fact that you are at the pharmacist, suggests precisely that everything is not okay. Moreover, Bas later clarifies, he does not go to the pharmacist as a context to engage in broad and deep personal conversations but to buy medication. Who is context blind then?

People—and specifically women—who were diagnosed at a later age, were for a long time able to conceal their autism by exhibiting socially desirable behaviour. With a few of the participants, this brought about questions about who they really are. Marie describes how she, when she was just diagnosed, could totally relate. It is for her "an explanation for weird traits, an overflowing and chaotic brain and a life wherein everything is complicated and difficult…" The diagnosis enables her to be more gentle to herself. With time, the doubts start to grow however: "… is the diagnosis correct, and if it is, I now know that what's wrong with me will always stay that way…" Marie describes how she mourns the fact that certain things will remain difficult. She has a great interest in other countries and cultures, but also an aversion to changes of scenery, which seriously complicates travelling for her. The diagnosis tells her that she will never be able to change this aspect of her personality. She also asks herself questions about her own identity. The diagnosis teaches her, namely, that adults, and mostly women, have learned to camouflage their issues and their identity:

> *On top of that, I ask myself even more than before WHO I am. Because if the diagnosis is correct, and I have been compensating, concealing and imitating behaviour my entire life: then who am I really? A collection of behaviours and attitudes that are a copy of others? I've quite the tendency to take over people's moods: what does that mean and why do I do that? Because I otherwise don't know how to behave? Because I'm oversensitive? What good is it to a sad friend that I also become sad……..? (I'm actually really bad at comforting)* [Marie]

Marie describes here, that if the diagnosis is correct and she really is autistic, that she has been able to cover that up her entire life. She also asks herself how she can still know herself. Kris has a similar observation:

> *Yeah, I keep having these questions: "who am I", right? I also met several autistic people who told me how they also worked with many adaptation strategies and adapt themselves a lot. That's something I really recognise. I actually really don't know who I am. I have always lived according to other people's expectations, according to what I thought the situation demanded. According to what they expected from me at school or at work, but I actually don't know who I am.* [Kris]

After a long period of suffering and adaptive behaviour, the diagnosis produces information to, again, start searching for who one really is. Els describes this feeling as if she has to rediscover herself:

> *Now, I just have to try to follow my feelings, I just have to try to reach that feeling. I've never done that in my life, and I am faced with very strange situations, strange questions: "Who am I then?" Actually, I don't know yet.* [Els]

In the quotation below, Sandra clearly tries to understand who she is in relation to the diagnosis:

> *In the beginning, it was a relief, you've got clarity after all. But I still haven't completely accepted it I think. I don't think that I will ever accept it but yeah, it's hard sometimes... It also depends on who you tell, right, not everyone understands to be honest. I also don't want to abuse the diagnosis or not even use it at all. But that diagnosis is important for me, for me as well as for the children actually. Not as a kind of excuse, but rather to get the assistance you are entitled to. That's what you need it for. However bad that is, but that's how it is, otherwise you're not entitled to home-based counselling. But as a person, I haven't changed, while I have noticed that once people – also people who know me very well – knew of the diagnosis, I was different to them. That I was different all of a sudden. Even though I have actually always been like that. I have always been confronted with these problems. But of course, from the moment you have that diagnosis, you have to deal with these prejudices.* [Sandra]

Throughout the entire conversation, Sandra emphasises that she is still the same person, that the diagnosis has not changed anything about that. The only difference is that her way of being has a name now. What *has* changed, is how people relate to her now. At another moment during the conversation, Sandra states that she is not only autistic, but that she is Sandra, a unique person whose autism is only one side of her.

In Chap. 5 (*Autism as a Way to Hold Your Own*), we have explained how a diagnosis can relieve feelings of guilt. The realisation that your shortcomings are due to a neurological 'being different' allows you to let go of certain issues. Does this mean, however, that you are from now on completely irresponsible for your actions? Baukis explains that even a diagnosis does not relieve you from being responsible for yourself. Here, she refers to raising her three sons. She has always given them the message that a diagnostic label is not something you can hide behind:

> *When you have an impairment (such as ASD for instance), this impairs what you can handle. The fact that you can't overstep your limits, is something no one can hold against you. Nevertheless, an impairment doesn't relieve you from the moral obligation to make the most of yourself. You don't have to do more, but you also shouldn't do less. You owe it to yourself and to the world. What you do with your life, within the limits of your possibilities, remains your own responsibility. You can demand your rights, but you will also still have obligations. Raising children means that you teach them that they have to take more and more responsibility for their own existence, and from your side as a parent it means that you have to grant your children more and more rights.* [Baukis]

We have mentioned a few times before that ASSpirin describes how she was convinced that she was difficult and antisocial before the diagnosis, and how people understand her more after the diagnosis. Still, this does not mean that now, she supposedly no longer has a choice, she writes:

> *But it remains a question of being and choice. The fact that there is a diagnosis doesn't mean that the choice is eliminated. No excuses, but interpretation.* [ASSpirin]

Does having a neurologically different brain mean that you are different or less responsible? In the quotation below, Tatiana describes how she questions the 'rock hard biological' aspect of autism. 'Biological' after all implies that it is hard to surpass, that it is rock hard. For herself, it remains a story however:

> *They no longer think vaccination could be a cause, but the idea that you can get it from something, for instance, from smoking, an older father, genetically in the family, that's logical of course, but I just think it's very difficult. I thought borderline was difficult, but that's psychology, that's just vague, but now they want to, they want to prove it genetically, biomedically. And then it becomes rock hard, and then it also is rock hard. And I think that's stupid. And because I don't know what it actually is, I also can't talk about it with other people. Because if they say what it is then, I first think to myself, it's just a story. Actually, I feel that from that moment, I'm telling a zero story.* [Tatiana]

Kris also experiences a certain discomfort with the vagueness of autism. How does such a general label relate to your own personality? 'Everyone is different', but there has to be a common element if we want to make a diagnosis:

I think it's all very fascinating, but it remains something very diverse and complex, everything that's involved with autism. Everyone is different and we all vary, also within autism. It's a spectrum, but that also makes it so difficult for me to actually capture like yeah, what is it actually. Because in order to give the definition, in order to be able to diagnose, there must be common elements, right. [Kris]

Carl doubts whether children who have not yet had to deal with a couple of obstacles should be diagnosed. After all, will they then not simply be regarded as a certain kind of person, which has quite a few consequences for their upbringing, treatment plans and special schooling. Should they not be regarded as a unique person? An adult is probably better able to handle this tension:

No, I don't think so, I think that, I'm really not sure about that. I think we do a better job by recognising the unicity of all human beings, and dealing with that, rather than sticking explanatory models or diagnoses onto it. It is true though, that these, these elements can help as thinking methods. But you have to let them go just as easily as you adopt them. [Carl]

Tatiana also has her doubts about the early diagnosis of children because diagnostic labels are too deterministic. Is it a good idea to tie children down to something, so early on? She explains that she is better able to assess the implications of the diagnosis than others… "because luckily, I'm just fifty, when I heard it, so I'm already pretty strong, but if I'd been twelve, it would have been a bit dangerous." Nora also suspects that there is a danger in early diagnoses:

A diagnosis can certainly help, but what can be dangerous, is that afterward, it's more difficult to think beyond a diagnosis. Not just the person itself, but also the people around this person should from time to time get the opportunity to move past it. Not to deny it, on the contrary, but moving past the formatting of a category, moving past it and being able to do your own thing with certain mapped out roads so that everyone can be just as entitled to doubts and risks. [Nora]

With an early diagnosis, so she says, there is the danger that children are no longer challenged to surpass themselves, and are brought up based on certain prescribed formulas that are available for a certain diagnosis.

BartDelam describes then that he would like to have his 15-year-old son tested as well. He recognises a lot of his own traits in him and regrets it very much that his autism was determined at such a late age:

I would like to have my son tested for autism as well because I recognise a lot of my traits in him. My therapist discourages this as long as my son does not display any problems. He is indeed doing well at school, not bullied, and there appear to be no other problems, but it is practically impossible to know what really goes on in his mind. He is very closed off and withdrawn. I hope he is not going down the same road as I did, where he first has to overstep his limits for years to eventually end up in a severe depression caused by exhaustion, before people consider a diagnosis. With a timely diagnosis, we could save him from a lot of trouble.
[BartDelam]

Our participants express an inherent ambiguity with respect to the diagnosis of autism. On the one hand, it offers an explanation and a possible way out of the existing problems. On the other hand, it is impossible to completely coincide with a phenomenon that is as heterogeneous as autism. The danger exists that you will regard yourself as defined solely by the diagnostic label. Not knowing can however sometimes result in unbearable suffering, which might have been prevented. Huws and Jones, who interviewed nine young people between 16 and 21 years old, also describe how a diagnosis can increase the self-esteem of the diagnosed person. Furthermore, a few of these people describe how their diagnosis decreased harassments, although some of them also explained that they were bullied precisely because of their diagnosis. The diagnosis has caused a disruption in the plans they made for themselves and their future, but has also offered an insight into new possibilities.[5]

It may be an odd principle, that we would write about accepting or not accepting a diagnosis that can clearly be determined and discerned. Still, our respondents sometimes doubt, criticise, are suspicious, besides also being respectful and appreciative of the diagnostic process. In that sense, it is clear that people have to accept that there is some truth to what was determined in the diagnostic process. Is it true that 'accepting' the diagnosis means that you accept a disorder which, according to certain interpretations, is a life sentence? The renewed engaging in new and further developments and learning from new experiences would then be almost futile, because it would eliminate autism. Meanings, mindsets, expectations about autism sometimes appear to be fixed and imposed by the immediate surroundings. This can stem from well-intended precaution, but also from incomprehension and inconvenience. The distinction that originates in formulating and discovering being different is therefore of

---

[5] Huws and Jones (2008).

vital importance, more than 'being autist'. Trying to put into words who you perceive yourself to be as a human being, also interpersonally, is not always easy. The amount of misconceptions and misunderstanding that the people you hold most dear can show can indeed start to dominate your own experience of who you are. In spite of the daily problems, many of our participants intuitively choose for the unknown and the full breadth of the developmental opportunities that keep emerging. It is often the setbacks, the obstacles, the challenges and the necessity to express oneself in conflict that lead(s) to learning. You can, for instance, learn who you are and how you can or should relate to the other. In Chap. 8 (*Perspectives on the Future*), we will further explore how our participants regard their lives after and with the diagnosis. How will they deal with feelings of acceptance and resistance toward this being different, while at the same time dealing with the sometimes disqualifying aspect of the diagnosis? How do *they* think about (health)care options?

Bibliography

Baron-Cohen, Simon. 1997. *Mindblindness: An Essay on Autism and Theory of Mind*. Cambridge, MA: MIT Press.

Huws, J.C., and R.S.P. Jones. 2008. Diagnosis, Disclosure, and Having Autism: An Interpretative Phenomenological Analysis of the Perceptions of Young People with Autism. *Journal of Intellectual & Developmental Disability* 33 (2): 99–107. Informa.

Lester, Jessica. 2012. A Discourse Analysis of Parents' Talk Around Their Children's Autism Labels. *Disability Studies Quarterly* 32 (4). The Ohio State University Libraries. http://dsq-sds.org/article/view/1744/3176.

Singh, Jennifer S. 2016. Parenting Work and Autism Trajectories of Care. *Sociology of Health & Illness* 38 (7): 1106–1120. Wiley.

CHAPTER 8

Perspectives on the Future

Abstract This chapter explores the perspectives people have on a future living with a diagnosis. A diagnosis implies a 'dysfunctioning', a label, a deficit, an 'abnormality'. How to think about the balance between finding recognition in the diagnosis on the one hand, but having to deal with the stigma society connects to the diagnosis on the other hand? Should you tell people or not? Do people still take you seriously after you tell them? Telling, for instance, your boss about your diagnosis can mean you receive some helpful benefits, but it can also lead to the fact that you are deemed unfit to perform certain tasks you consider yourself perfectly fit to perform. This chapter also deals with how society sometimes tends to patronise people with a diagnosis, while this is certainly not what they ask for.

Keywords Autism • Future • Employment • Relationships

A diagnosis of autism can help to get recognition for certain sensitivities others do not perceive. People can, for instance, have legitimate reasons to avoid an overload of noise and sound. We can think of other kinds of labels: it is very accepted that someone with the label *photographer* has an eye for light intensity. It is also accepted that someone with the label *painter* sees more or identifies more colours. Autistic people share a similar experience, and their diagnosis can help others realise how they can take the person in question into account. Given the heterogeneity of autism, it sometimes remains unclear what people exactly have to make room for when dealing with someone who has the diagnosis. Moreover, autism is associated with dysfunctioning. The danger in this is that people are not completely taken seriously anymore. Just as in the Middle Ages, missing a hand or an arm or any other physical defect was regarded as a sign of the devil, today, the term 'autism' for some people still means a serious and peculiar disorder people cannot really make sense of. In other words, a diagnosis offers a helping hand, but also has several, far-reaching consequences on a social level. This is exactly why five of our interviewees struggle with the question whether or not they should inform their employer about their diagnosis.

After the diagnosis, a new task commences: *relating* to the diagnosis. The sole explanation from the diagnostician about what to expect is not enough. A diagnosis is welcomed as an explanatory model for previous problems, but it should also offer a way out of the impasse many of our people reside in at the moment they decide to get diagnosed. A diagnosis by a psychiatrist also provides entitlement to compensations and support, more so than for instance when someone has a hypersensitive personality: a diagnosis allows you to stop participating in busy life for a while. In this chapter, we describe how autism works in social relations and in the job market. We also elaborate on the role of the social institutions after the diagnosis.

The respondents who are in a relationship often speak very respectfully about their partners. They often call this person one of the most important people in their lives, because most of the time, they manage to take the peculiarities of the respondents into consideration and act accordingly. The clarification the diagnosis of autism offers is often also useful for the people around the diagnosed person, and it can help these people deal with this 'being different':

Yeah I do think for myself… Well it's a double-edged sword, it's difficult on the one hand but it also makes things easier on the other hand. Now, my boyfriend or my parents say, oh yeah well this happens because of that, while before the diagnosis, these same things used to escalate into a fight. She can't help it, so to speak, so we'll just leave it as it is. [Hannah]

Now that the diagnosis has been made, Sofie, for example, has a desire to get in contact with other people with a diagnosis of autism, to talk to them about the problems and how they deal with them:

For instance, in The Netherlands, there is a pub for autistic people, and I'm like, I would like to get in contact with adults, with normal intelligence as well of course, who also have autism, to talk about the issues they deal with. [Sofie]

Hannah sometimes works at the reception for the doctor who was part of the facility she was diagnosed in. When she does this, she also meets other autistic people, and notices how much understanding there is in an environment with others who are dealing with a similar problem:

When I'm in that context, I feel that the people there are different, and that there is a lot of understanding and that I can be myself there so much more. So if the world would be more like that, for people like me – of whom I'm convinced that there are a lot more – life would be easier. Then these people would dare to express themselves a lot more as well, and perhaps they would also dare to say what they think more. But I think that the world isn't ready yet, and that it is still going to take a very long time. I don't think, I don't feel that I will live to see the day, but maybe someday that day will come. [Hannah]

A bit further in the interview, Hannah explains that sharing a diagnosis does not necessarily mean you feel a connection with that person:

... sometimes people also think that, oh yeah, they both have autism, I'm sure... but that's also just a person like any other, that doesn't mean you have a connection... [Hannah]

A question on a few of the participants' minds is whether they should tell a few people outside their immediate surroundings about the diagnosis. Albert explains that he would lose credibility in his job as a family doctor. That is why he thinks really well about who he tells and who he does not tell:

The fear that I will no longer be taken seriously (which would be very difficult for a general practitioner) and the incomprehension it would provoke. I'm not yet sure at all whether I should keep the diagnosis to myself or share it. Sometimes I do feel the desire to share the diagnosis and I do share this carefully, with people I have selected in advance. [Albert]

Robyn says the diagnosis and the explanation she was given about the diagnosis helped her explain her uniqueness to others:

Most people were like, this can't be, but when I let them read the report, they understood. Because that was the most important thing for me, the report, because I was never really able to explain what my problems were. And that little package, that was a bit like, voila, these are my problems, just read that and then you know. And that was really a relief for me, like voila, now I no longer have to try to explain that, but people can just read that and then they'll begin to understand. [Robyn]

For Robyn, the diagnosis and the diagnostic report serve as guidelines with her problems. Since the diagnosis, she is able to make clear what is going on with her because of how it is written down.

Although a diagnosis of autism can serve as an explanatory model in itself, participants sometimes indicate that not much is being done with the data that were generated from the tests. Carl says: "Yeah not that, just that the world of the diagnosis is hyper flat." Even though the tests often indicate very specific cognitive abilities and deficits, this does not necessarily mean that this collection of data is actually used effectively. During the interview, Michael repeatedly refers to the time and money that is invested in the tests, but that nothing is done with the results:

> *Yeah you often just get a score, and then you've got ASD or Asperger's or I don't know what, but what you're bothered about the most, which parts, and what did you do wrong there, that you can learn something from that about how you specifically should handle things. But they don't do that.* [Michael]

In Belgium, a diagnosis does not mean that you automatically get the appropriate care. One of the possibilities that autistic people have is that they can make an appeal for an autism coach. This is someone who guides and supports children or adults, and who helps them discover their possibilities and develop their talents. Although there are courses to become an autism coach, it is not a protected title and there are no specific requirements regarding degrees you need to qualify. The care this autism coach offers will therefore not always be refunded by your insurance company.

Sofie was given her diagnosis two-and-a-half weeks before the conversation with us. She has good hopes that the person she contacted, a remedial educationalist who is specialised in autism, will mentor her concerning certain behaviours and habits that are difficult for her:

> *I don't know if that's different, but I do run into this. That if someone hurts me, it feels as if a slow train comes crashing in. And she said, I've heard the same from some other autistic people. I didn't know that was the case, because you don't know these things. For instance when I'm overstimulated, that I – for me it feels that way – immediately go from zero to ten… It's as if there's no transition between these two extremes. For instance when someone's tapping their fingers on the table, I can only think like: "stop it, stop it, stop it", and then I can only say to that person: "STOP IT." I don't know how to say that in a modest way, because my fuses blow. When that person stops, I immediately go back to zero, but when he starts again, I'm immediately at ten. She [the coach, KH] is going to teach me how to sense this sooner, and tell me how I can anticipate that…* [Sofie]

Samuel gives a description of what he considers to be a good autism coach. He also mentions that a tricky issue is the fact that traditionally, counsellors have the most experience with people with a mental disability:

> *A good autism coach is someone who works solution-oriented. Who begins with what works, and then searches, together with the person, for what can be better in his or her life, and what bothers him or her. People such as myself, in the sense of my intelligence, and who are perhaps a bit more critical than on average... Yeah, there is a very outdated image, that focuses on people with a slight mental disability, with limited communication abilities and little insight into their own autism.* [Samuel]

For Bas, a good counsellor is someone who is able to translate between the inner world of autists and the inner world of non-autists. His or her task is then to function as an interpreter. He explains that 'understanding' autism on a theoretical level is not enough:

> *What do people need? That's the issue, right. Yeah, sometimes I think: I would just need to have someone with me for a week, a kind of interpreter, who can dialogue between the NT world and the autism world. Who, with everything I do, would say like: "look, he is going to expect that, if you just do this, you can accomplish that. If you say that, you'll make yourself unsympathetic, etcetera. If you just fix it like that, it'll be fixed nice and diplomatically." Yeah, that would actually be good.* [Bas]

Marie also says she would like to have someone explain certain things to her, things that are different with her:

> *I sought (and seek) help, amongst other things, not just because I want to understand why I'm so overstimulated all the time or why I have problems with change and surprises, why I sometimes develop strange eating habits, or that I almost always notice it when a painting has been moved or removed. It goes beyond that: I don't know who I am and sometimes I also don't know how I should behave in certain social situations which others would label as 'normal'. Which behaviour is specifically me and which behaviour is learned or copied? If I seek help for everything because I want to understand who I am in order to avoid a new identity crisis (and depression), I expect information and not smiling psychiatrists who supposedly know best.* [Marie]

Tatiana explains that she receives good help from someone who also has a diagnosis of Asperger's syndrome. She concludes: "I would like it if more of my counsellors were autists. That's secretly the kind of help I want." She would also like to start a study so she can eventually help people with a diagnosis of autism herself.

Robyn, and Sandra, Marie, Hannah, Samuel and Albert too, found a good counsellor after the diagnosis. Matteo explains that, because of his diagnosis, he is entitled to a job coach who helps him find a job. Samuel tells us that financial obstacles can, however, prevent you from meeting the autism coach as often as you would like. He says that he meets with his coach once a month, although it would actually be better if he had four appointments in a month. He cannot afford that financially. Sandra describes the difference between the family worker of her children and other counsellors she has met:

> *And I think it's because of the direct communication, because he is just so direct and so honest, and that I'm just who I am and he's not constantly interpreting my behaviour. For instance, with a few counsellors who don't have autism, I have the feeling that I have to explain myself, that I have to justify why I'm saying that or doing this. Or that they think there's more to it than meets the eye. Sometimes I don't know anymore what's expected of me. He doesn't have autism himself, but I don't have that with him. That's quite important: if you need counsellors, you have to look for the good ones.* [Sandra]

Later in the conversation, Sandra further clarifies:

> *A counsellor doesn't have to have ASD in order to be able to understand me. It's about personality, letting someone be who he is. I'm convinced that there are also counsellors that are experts on autism, who don't always do the right thing. It can be a pitfall when you know a lot about ASD and then to think you really understand that person with ASD. It is indeed quite important that you look for counsellors that suit you, with whom you feel good and that you don't just take an autism specialist, because it's a specialist. You must surround yourself with the right caregivers for YOU, who is a good counsellor for YOU!* [Sandra]

Still, not everyone is happy with the help they got. Els describes her counselling as very patronising:

> *Yeah, that counselling, it wasn't very good. She's very patronising. She is more focused on autistic people who are more dependent. As if that therapist also wanted to make me depend on her, as if she had to be a friend for me. Perhaps I judged it incorrectly, but she kept wanting to talk about things that aren't a problem for me. I said three times already that I wasn't going to go there anymore, and still I went, every time… I didn't have an alternative. I just told her, look, when I'm with you I don't say the things I actually planned to say. But she kept curious about things that weren't important to me. She sometimes already*

> concluded things before I did, and in the beginning that may have been easy for her because she already knows a lot and has experience. But she takes these conclusions as a starting point and then they're also not always correct or they are correct but of marginal importance to me, while there are other issues that are more important to me, but which I don't seem to be able to address. The books I read, the congresses and lectures I go to and the conversations I have with other autistic people help me much more. [Els]

Els explains that she hopes that contact with likeminded people, with other autistic women for instance, will help her more than the guidance she has had so far.

Baukis tells us that the model of the Flemish Autism Association is a good example of how autistic people should be approached:

> The VVA often functions as a model to show what a good way of working is for people who need care. I think that's absolutely correct: their starting point is very much who you are, what you ask, what you can handle, and they definitely don't overlook your strong points. I think that's very important, because well, there is a lot that you're not or less able to do, but there's also a lot that you can do, and let's just continue from that. When you can't go to school (anymore) for instance, we will scale it back to a level that's doable for you, and from there we'll start building up again. We'll see how far we get. We work with our strong points. And I think that's a good way of working. The first and most important thing is respect for the person who sits there. Please don't forget that, that you're dealing with people and that every person – however limited – has feelings and deserves to be treated with respect. [Baukis]

Baukis indicates that this model is based on respect and underlines the importance thereof in relation to the other. Respect offers an opening towards recognising everyone's personal ability to act and to judge.

For some respondents, the diagnosis offers the necessary social protection and support. The diagnosis has, for BartDelam, enabled him to start working part-time. Els is on sick leave, and is not sure if she wants to go back to her toxic work environment. Samuel explains how his partner, who also has autism, is excused from the obligation to attend office parties. Bas identifies two advantages of having a diagnosis of autism: on the one hand, it has confirmed his hypothesis. On the other hand, it is a legitimising factor on the job market:

> I wanted to refer to, call it the legitimising factor, where it's difficult in many areas, including the job market… Yeah, you can also benefit from your diagnosis

right, in relation to the state. People at the RVA [Rijksdienst voor Arbeidsvoorziening, the Belgian National Employment Service, KH] will react differently for instance, when you say it's autism, than when that's not the case. There's also an explanatory factor in it. And I have no scruples about it, because I know that the disadvantage I experience from autism is still much bigger than the few advantages, right. And unemployment in itself, with all its implications, still remains an immense disadvantage for many autistic people. Others seldom take us into account, but we do have to take someone else into account, day in and day out. And then they tell us that we so stubbornly hold on to our own principles etcetera. So that's also not fair at all. [Bas]

A few participants hesitate to tell others that they have a diagnosis. Hannah says that a diagnosis will not be accepted at all at work. Michael, who is looking for a more permanent solution than the flexi-jobs he is doing at the moment, says it is better to use a different diagnosis, NLD, because it is more socially accepted. As mentioned several times before, autism is generally associated with isolated, socially inhibited and eccentric personality traits.

Sandra did share her diagnosis at work. This disclosure, however, resulted in her work no longer allowing her to perform a few of her previous tasks.

People say, you'll not be able to do this, and that... That was just immediately decided, in my place, or things were radically extended. While, okay, contact with people in my job, that's very difficult, but I've always done that perfectly well, but it is quite tiring. And yeah, it actually made me sick a bit, you have to put a lot of energy into that. But to say like, you've got autism, okay, no more customer contact at all ... [Sandra]

Sandra feels that her employers were too quick to judge when they decided that she should no longer get in contact with clients:

I also say that: the others have more problems with me than I have with them, I think. I also often say to those people like, if you think or feel that, that says more about you than about me. People of course don't really like it when you say that, but it's true. And yeah, ever since I got the diagnosis, people sometimes start to think in my place and will unravel entire theories. But I'm often like, yeah, but all of that isn't right. That's quite frustrating, that's tiring. In that sense, I do recognise that, that they shouldn't want to take over everything, they just have to let me be who I am, right. That would be the easiest. [Sandra]

Michael has had similar experiences. He received special education as a child, and vocational education afterwards. Now, he is looking for a job that suits him. He is counselled by a psychologist and he has a job coach, but he thinks it is a pity that they—in spite of all the tests—do not seem to be able to use this data to find him an appropriate job. After the diagnosis, he once told someone he has autism, and his experience was similar to Sandra's:

> *And then I'm not even allowed to do most activities because people think I can't handle it. I'm indeed not capable of certain things, but people don't often ask me what's difficult for me for instance. Or what can we do and what can't we do. And we could supposedly talk things through together, but like not really... People also don't make time for that, and a job coach will also not come visit but... You can't explain that they have the wrong impression of it. Then I think, I can be social, I can do that, and then you try to explain that a bit, but...*
> [Michael]

At another point in the conversation, Michael says that people treat him like a child when he tells them he has a diagnosis. According to him, telling people that you have a diagnosis of autism runs the risk of people solely looking at you in light of a stereotypical image which is connected to the diagnosis. People, for instance, also assume that he is not able to do certain things, and that he will, therefore, never do them again. In the context of individual job guidance, Michael has done several tests to decide what could be an appropriate job for him. He is very disappointed, however, that the results of these tests have not been used:

> *When we started, I had to do several tasks and I have an entire report about it, but then they didn't do anything with it. Then they just say: "They're looking for people there, why don't you start working there." They did make a work schedule I think, but other than that they didn't look any further. And that's what they're for normally, those tests, to test certain jobs and all. Yeah. And then to afterwards look what did they see and what has happened in the job... And then I think, why did you make me do an assessment to begin with, to eventually not use much from it at all.* [Michael]

On a personal level, the future for our respondents may not be simple, but it is possible to gain an overview and a future is conceivable from an open developmental perspective. Socially, however, and in relation to work—more specifically the finding of work or not or being able to function in the workplace or not—it is still complex sometimes. Our respondents do offer suggestions as to how they could be put on their way. They are looking for help—and some have already found it—to better understand communication. The quest for tools that could make their daily life easier leads for example to usable information about sleeping hygiene or about self-organisation.

In their qualitative research on anxieties in young adults with autism, Trembath and colleagues found, for instance, meditation techniques ('grounding oneself'), which some counsellors apply to help this target audience deal with their anxieties.[1] By disclosing your diagnosis as an adult, however, you inevitably run into dominant prejudices. Fear of prejudices can lead to the decision to remain silent about a diagnosis.

In a study about the experiences of 12 students with a diagnosis of autism at universities in the United States, Wiorkowski describes how disclosing your diagnosis can lead to certain assumptions with administrative or teaching staff. More specifically, it leads to judgments about what this target group can or cannot do. As a consequence, the facilities that are offered to people with a diagnosis are not always perceived positively. As an example, examinations provided for this target group, in separate test rooms and outside teaching hours, are perceived as difficult by the people concerned.[2] Our interviewees describe these possibilities as limitations to their professional lives. They indicate that they would prefer to not to go too far in adapting to their diagnosis in order to prevent confrontations, since a confrontation also offers them the possibility to learn.

Bibliography

Trembath, D., C. Germano, G. Johanson, and C. Dissanayake. 2012. The Experience of Anxiety in Young Adults With Autism Spectrum Disorders. *Focus on Autism and Other Developmental Disabilities* 27 (4): 213–224. Sage Publications.

Wiorkowski, F. 2015. The Experiences of Students with Autism Spectrum Disorders in College: A Heuristic Exploration. *The Qualitative Report* 20 (6): 847. Nova Southeastern University.

---

[1] Trembath et al. (2012).
[2] Wiorkowski (2015).

CHAPTER 9

Afterthoughts

Abstract What is autism? With this study, we have chosen to open up the space of interpretation by using the spoken words of our respondents. We used a phenomenological approach by asking questions regarding (the interpretation of) personal experiences. In drawing up the questions as in the analysis of the theoretical explanatory models of autism, we have given the story of the respondent—diagnosed with autism as an adult—a central role. Especially the variety of—and not the similarity between—experiences of people with an autism diagnosis has been given a platform in this book. Our study shows that the issue may perhaps not really be what the essence of autism actually is, but rather how it works as a concept. If we can grasp how something works, it eventually also teaches us something about what it actually is.

Keywords Communication • Dynamics • Interaction • Sensory differences

Throughout the years, the question "What is autism?" has been answered by psychologists, psychiatrists, genetics and neurologists in several and very diverse ways. After decades of genetic and neurological research, biology has—up until this day—not yet provided us with a univocal cause of autism. It seems clear that there is something different in the brains of people with a diagnosis of autism, but what that could be and where exactly this difference is to be located remain difficult to grasp. Given the many and at times contradictory scientific findings, it is sometimes suggested that autism does not really exist, or that autism is merely a linguistic construct, lacking an underlying essence. With this study, we have chosen not to engage in this discussion, but rather to open up the space of interpretation with the spoken words of our respondents. Following the hermeneutic outlook of the philosopher Wilhelm Dilthey, this study does not wish to enter the realm of explanations (*what is autism really?*) but rather the realm of understanding.[1] We have asked our target group the following questions: "What does it mean to receive a diagnosis of autism when you are an adult?", "Does a diagnosis help to see your own being different in another perspective?", "Is 'autism' a sufficient explanation?", "Does the meaning of autism merely lie in the instrumental – with this diagnostic label, I will have access to more facilities and understanding at work and with my family – or do you also really learn something about the way you function in daily life?" We used a phenomenological approach by asking questions regarding (the interpretation of) personal experiences. We consciously placed the quest for an explanation about the phenomenon autism outside the setup of our research. In drawing up the questions as in the analysis of the theoretical explanatory models of autism, we have given the story of the respondent—diagnosed with autism at a later age—a central role. Especially the variety of—and not the similarities between—experiences of people diagnosed with autism has been given a platform in this book.

In these afterthoughts, we want to take a moment to look at several 'common threads' which we have noticed during our analyses of the interviews. We are aware of the fact that generalising personal experiences of 21 people is impossible. Moreover, there has surely been some bias in our selection. Our participants signed up in order to tell their stories about their experiences. They are people who were diagnosed as an adult and who are able to express themselves in spoken or written language. People sometimes appealed to other forms of expression, such as image, dance and music. We did not solicit diagnostic reports in order to prevent our own impressions to be influenced by certain data about processing speed, IQ etcetera. Moreover, it is not the intention of a qualitative study to generalise findings in the first place.

We have noticed some similarities between personal stories. Our respondents often recount stories about sensory overstimulation, which can become so all-encompassing that it can severely complicate their daily routine. Several respondents also told us about feeling overloaded in the past,

[1] Dilthey (1990).

because they were taking on a lot more than they could handle. The intensity of perceiving reality, deeply and specifically thinking through (the event of) that reality—far more intensely than what is socially accepted—is something that came up many times in many of the interviews. Noticing things that others might miss or ignore can certainly have its advantages in certain work environments and can even be a lifesaver. It can, however, also lead to people getting lost in details, which inhibits them from moving forward. The question remains whether this way of thinking means you de facto get stuck, or that our society should make room for people who want to dwell a bit longer on certain things they encounter. Both at work, as everywhere else, everything must progress quickly. That is why we perhaps too easily expect people to just work with limited instructions, superficialities and presumptions. We notice, however, that our participants simply have no other option than to seek out and notice certain nuances. Perhaps people need more room to be able to take time and dwell on certain issues. Instead of using the diagnosis to problematise a certain person and his/her behaviour, it should be used as a starting point to better analyse the context in terms of strengths and problems. How did people deal with the problems they experience and the problems their surroundings experience up until now? What can be done about this, taking strengths and weaknesses into account?

Whether autism is essentially a difference in processing information or whether it is first and foremost a deficit in social interaction is still a topic of discussion among autism researchers. More recent theories, such as the Intense World Theory[2] or the High, Inflexible Precision of Prediction Errors (HIPPEA)[3] suggest exactly that social interaction is hindered by underlying differences and problems in sensory and information processing in general. In this light, it is even more remarkable that our participants explicitly emphasise their social mindset. Many of them stress that they have a need for regular, good conversations that go beyond the superficial 'chitchat' level. Our respondents have to contend with the preconception that autistic people are less empathetic or that they care less about others. Some of our respondents tell us extensive stories about their issues regarding certain communicative misunderstandings. It seems only logical that—when you keep running into these misunderstandings—you

---

[2] Markram, Rinaldi and Markram (2007).
[3] Van de Cruys et al. (2014).

would eventually prefer to withdraw from social interactions. Still, people indicate that they also want to learn to communicate in such a way that they can come to a mutual understanding.

It may be useful to think about what it actually means to 'understand an other'. There is an increasing amount of knowledge available about how brains develop dynamically. We should also begin to understand communication and social skills in a more intersubjective way, as an active interplay between individuals. For instance, how normal it is when a person asks an additional question that the other has no patience for that or that he is reluctant to further examine the issue that is raised. Perhaps this is about dynamics which are and remain important throughout people's lives. We recognised, in our participants, a will to communicate with the other, but because people are stuck in their preconceptions or are overwhelmed by impressions that are considered to be of secondary importance, it just sometimes does not work. Conflicts and misunderstandings can, however, also be a motivation to learn actively. The fact that our participants have somehow been able to persevere throughout their lives is a sign of resilience and suggests at least that there is a possibility and a will to learn and to develop. Although a diagnosis of autism can be interpreted as a certain judgement about communicative qualities, it apparently does not have to be that way. It can offer insight into where things go wrong, and because of that it can be an opening to gain a mutual understanding. What follows are adaptations and clarifications in communication. This is of course only possible if the diagnosis is regarded as a starting point for approaching one another, and not as a label and package of measures to remain standing. It is not about creating separate worlds for several kinds of people, but about emphasising the learning effect of confrontations in the analysis.

Besides disclosing our respondents' struggles and experiences of being different, we have also tried to illustrate how people have experienced the diagnostic process and the diagnosis itself. After all, *they* had questions about themselves and how they function in society, and *they* have decided— often after a long period of suffering—to get tested for autism. Some of them immediately identified with the diagnosis, in some cases initially via the diagnosis of their children, for others the suggestion to get tested came as more of a surprise. For many, recognition came after the diagnosis, even though some have doubts about the validity of the tests or about stereotypical representations of autism in general. For most of our respondents, autism offers the best description of their being different they have heard of, so far. We do see many similarities with the concept of moral career as described by Erving Goffman, for instance, in his books *Stigma* and *Asylums*.[45] He writes that:

> Persons who have a particular stigma tend to have similar learning experiences regarding their plight, and similar changes in conceptions of self – a similar 'moral career' that is both cause and effect of commitment to a similar sequence of personal adjustments.[6]

With stigma, Goffman refers to traits or circumstances that make someone different than others, and in that respect also a bit conspicuous. This can be a physical handicap, an addiction, a certain social status or a psychiatric diagnosis. The—possibly—new identity as provided by for instance a diagnosis, makes people look at themselves differently.

Our participants also tell us that the diagnosis provides a certain insight which makes them regard the problems they had earlier on in their lives, differently and anew. Some participants regard the diagnostic process with a certain detachment, while others emphasise the scientific objectivity of the tests. There is not one interviewee who does not have their own opinion about his or her condition and problems. This personal judgement is at least as important as the diagnosis itself. An official diagnosis is mainly necessary in order to make one's own judgement come across as trustworthy, for the respondents themselves but also for the people around them. And even though all respondents always kind of knew that they functioned differently in certain areas than other people, the diagnosis of autism also provides words for what exactly *is* the matter. How you think about yourself also depends on the words that are available. In this respect, a diagnosis of autism is similar to what Ian Hacking described as a "looping effect"[7]: the classification changes the classified, but also the other way around. Because people do not completely fit in certain categories, their experiences will also begin to influence the categories. An example thereof is the addition of sensory differences in DSM-5: because autistic people have indicated this as the core of their experiences, this has eventually become a part of the classification system. People with a diagnosis of autism will

[4] Goffman (1990).
[5] Goffman (1963).
[6] Idem. p. 45.
[7] Hacking (1996).

hopefully get more and more room to share their own experiences, and will thus participate in a further development and understanding of the meaning of autism.

A majority of our participants had already received other diagnoses: borderline personality disorder, obsessive-compulsive disorder, learning disorders such as non-verbal learning disorder… Nevertheless, most of our respondents consider the diagnosis of autism to be the most real and final. We think that this has to do with the fact that autism is considered to be more 'real' than, for instance, personality disorders. Autism is something that is embedded in your brain, your biology. On top of that, research on finding the biological (genetical, neurological) cause of autism, is currently receiving more financing than research on other psychiatric diagnoses. Autism is how you are *wired*, and in that respect this diagnosis relieves you of perfectionism, even more so than other diagnoses. Before the diagnosis, some of our participants used to set very high standard for themselves, standards they were often not able to live up to. The diagnosis is for them a sign that they can or do not have to do this anymore. Autism is also a very heterogeneous phenomenon. Something is wrong inside your brain, but since autism is now considered to be a very broad spectrum, it is not necessary to completely coincide with the stereotypical image. It is perfectly possible and not contradictory to say that you are autistic, but at the same time extremely empathetic. Or that you have problems understanding or assessing the other, but that you do think that you can still learn a lot in that area. This is why a diagnosis is not a strict mould from which you cannot escape, but rather a guiding beacon that indicates what is easy and what can (still) be difficult.

What does autism mean? How should we ethically handle diagnoses? We agree with Richard Rorty, when he says—referring to Gadamer's *wirkungsgeschichtliches Bewusstsein*—that what we need is "an attitude interested not so much in what is out there in the world, or what happened in history, as in what we can get out of nature and history for our own uses." He continues: "In this attitude, getting the facts right (about atoms and the void, or about the history of Europe) is merely propaedeutic to finding a new and more interesting way of expressing ourselves, and thus of coming with the world."[8] Our study shows that the issue may perhaps not really be what the essence of autism actually *is*, but rather how it *works* as a concept. If we can grasp how something works, it eventually

---

[8] Rorty (1980).

also teaches us something about what it actually is. This does not mean, however, that we can just decide what autism really is and what it is not by ourselves, or that it would be something entirely subjective. The experiences of being different, to which our people testify, are most definitely real, and often shared as well. Research on autism, and on human experience in general, should, besides *explaining*, be more focused on *understanding*. Several participants have, after their diagnosis, tried to understand how they could *learn* while interacting. Some of them have, for instance, learned to interrupt themselves when they notice that they are getting stuck or are overreacting. This is no different for people without a diagnosis of autism however. They too can, while interacting with those who function differently on a neurological level, learn to adapt their own expectations and behaviour. Understanding is after all by definition intersubjective.

We hope that this study has given an insight into how autism as a diagnosis has been a help to people who, at a certain moment in their lives, have encountered certain challenges. We would, therefore, plead for an approach to autism that is not so much affirmative and dogmatic, but rather investigative and dynamic. The testimonies of our participants show the possibilities of such an approach to research.

BIBLIOGRAPHY

Dilthey, Wilhelm. 1990. Ideen Über Eine Beschreibende Und Zergliedernde Psychologie (1894). In: *Die Geistige Welt*, 139–240. Gesammelte Schriften, Vol. 5. Vandenhoeck & Ruprecht.

Goffman, Erving. 1963. *Stigma. Notes on the Management of Spoiled Identity.* Englewood Cliffs: Prentice Hall.

Goffman, Erving. 1990. *Asylums: Essays on the Social Situation of Mental Patients and Other Inmates.* New York: Anchor Books.

Hacking, Ian. 1996. The Looping Effects of Human Kinds. In *Causal Cognition*, ed. Dan Sperber, David Premack, and Ann James Premack, 351–383. New York: Oxford University Press.

Markram, H., Tania Rinaldi, and Kamila Markram. 2007. The Intense World Syndrome – An Alternative Hypothesis for Autism. *Frontiers in Neuroscience* 1 (1): 77–96. Frontiers media, October 15.

Rorty, Richard. 1980. *Philosophy and the Mirror of Nature.* Princeton: Princeton University Press.

Van de Cruys, Kris Evers Sander, Ruth Van der Hallen, Lien Van Eylen, Bart Boets, Lee de-Wit, and Johan Wagemans. 2014. Precise Minds in Uncertain Worlds: Predictive Coding in Autism. *Psychological Review* 121 (4): 649–675. American Psychological Association, October.

Appendix: The Helping Thoughts of BartDelam

Helping thoughts are words or short sentences that help me skip the usual extensive and inefficient stream of thoughts in order to come to a quicker and better decision or result.

Helping thoughts are a technique for me to compensate for the negative consequences that result from the different way of processing information that is typical of ASD. Examples of this are a slower processing of information, the processing of details, the desire for clarity and predictability, the lack of imagination, rigidity, problems with the regulation of emotions, lack of empathetic abilities, problems with planning, context blindness, but also secondary problems such as anxiety, stress, a negative self-image, fallacies, perfectionism, worrying, a lack of assertiveness, a lack of initiative, social anxiety, annoyances and conflicts.

Helping thoughts prevent short circuiting in my thoughts. Because of ASD, many of my cognitive processes are not sensitive or intuitive, something which NT people often do have. Instead, all cognitive processes have to be reasoned rationally. First and foremost, this requires more time. There are also many senseless and inefficient detailed thoughts associated with this, which prevents people from seeing the main issue. It becomes a chaos of thoughts, which eventually leads to a short circuit. When that happens, I am no longer able to think straight and it is no longer possible to achieve results.

Some helping thoughts are similar to clichés (something that has been said so often that it no longer means a lot), but to me, they are not clichés at all. It is not some little story I tell myself to gather strength, because when I do not really believe it, it does not have any effect.

The helping thought is a kind of short summary (existing of one word or one sentence) of a previously reasoned line of thinking. When the cognitive processes fall short, the helping thought helps me to skip the complex line of thinking in order to come to a result much quicker. Thus, behind each helping thought, there is an extensively reasoned line of thinking.

What can be a helping thought to me does not have to be one for everyone. People with a different personality can sometimes benefit from an opposite thought.

In order to be able to use the helping thoughts, it is very important to recognise, in time, the situations wherein these thoughts can be used. For autistic people, it is not obvious to make contact with their own feelings and problems and to ascribe the correct meaning to them. Along the way, I have trained myself to recognise those situations and to evoke the correct helping thought in time. For me, they are immensely important, as they enable me to quicker and better deal with the problems which arise from the fact that I process information differently.

Examples of helping thoughts:
Strange
Source: my own finding
Helps me to get more in touch with my feelings, and to deal with unexpected issues in relation to others better.

Background: in social situations, it very often occurs that something happens which I did not expect; for instance, an unfriendly response, manipulation, an unexpected proposal… I often do not realise what is happening. It gives me a 'strange' feeling and a sense that something is not right (the way I thought about it), but I do not exactly know what it is. It makes me more insecure about how I should deal with it. Only afterwards, when I rethink the situation, I notice that something happened that I did not want. At that moment, I feel confused and powerless. Afterwards, it feels as if I fell into a trap. When I manage to connect this uncomfortable feeling to the helping thought 'strange', I realise at that moment that something is happening to me but I do not exactly know what it is. My most suitable response then is to win time, so I can reason what is happening and what the best reaction would be.

Take a Step Back
Source: my own finding
Helps me to return from the details to the main issue.

Background: in conversations with others, as well as in my own thoughts, I often get entangled in useless details. While discussing with others, I also easily let myself get trapped in a distraction towards a detail which has almost nothing to do with the main issue. When I feel that I am going to get trapped therein, these helping thoughts can help me to 'reset' the thought process to return to the main issue.

Don't Think, Do
Source: relaxation therapist
Helps me to stop putting off little tasks and, therefore, helps me to come to a result much quicker.

Background: in order to be able to start something, the task must be completely clear in advance, often in detail. I have to be able to imagine all the steps of the task and all possible problems must be eliminated beforehand.

With more complex or new tasks, it is virtually impossible to have a clear view of the entire script in advance, which results in not getting started on the task.

With the helping thought 'don't think, do', I can convince myself to start the task anyway, even if not everything is clear in advance. I know that it is impossible to foresee everything. I no longer have to overthink all options and consequences in detail. By beginning with the task, I come to results much quicker. By starting the task, the next steps become clear by themselves, as it were. The full task is automatically divided in subtasks. Instead of having to have the subtasks clear in advance, clarification now comes while executing the task. I also know now that problems can always arise, but when that happens I will try to solve them at that moment (instead of beforehand).

We Will Solve the Problems When They Arise
Source: Jean-Luc Dehaene[1]
Helps me to let myself be guided less by all that can go wrong. It helps me to stop putting off little tasks and, therefore, to come to a result much quicker.

---

[1] Prime-minister of Belgium 1992–1999.

Background: this helping thought is in line with the helping thought 'don't think, do'. Just as everything has to be clear in advance, I have the tendency to want to foresee and solve all possible problems beforehand. This thought process slows everything down, which results in the fact that eventually nothing happens. In the meantime, I also realise that only a fraction of the foreseen problems will ever become reality. For less important issues, it is therefore better for me if I let go trying to predict and solve all possible problems beforehand.

It's not Amputating a Leg
Source: relaxation therapist
Helps me to be less perfectionistic and to make a distinction between the important and the less important issues.

Background: in everything I did, I tried to be as perfectionist as possible. I certainly did not want to make mistakes. Everything was equally important. The relaxation therapist pointed the importance of seeing something in the right context out to me. A surgeon who has to amputate a leg should under no circumstance amputate the wrong leg. An entrepreneur who has to pay a bill of several millions of euros, better not pay this bill twice. Hence the helping thought: 'it's not amputating a leg'. The things I do are never as big as amputating a leg. With the work I usually do, I am allowed to make a (small) mistake once or twice. And if there is a mistake somewhere, it can usually still be corrected (contrary to the wrong amputated leg). I, therefore, no longer have to think that everything is equally important, and am allowed to be happy with a normal satisfying result.

Says Who?
Source: relaxation therapist
Helps me to get in touch with my feelings, to be less perfectionist, to consider the context better and to take more distance from rituals.

Background: because of my autism, I have a strong tendency to hold on to all sorts of little rules. I have incorporated those rules along the way. They are often very strict and detailed. They tell me what and how I should do everything. I often no longer know where these rules came from, but my inner voice (inner critic) keeps repeating them. These lead to perfectionism (to live by all those rules), fear of losing control (because I expect others to apply those rules as well) and discontent or a feeling of failure (because I eventually do not manage to apply all these rules). When I notice again that something has to go the way I want, the helping thought 'says who' helps me question the rule. Is it really so important that it happens my way, in other words, am I really convinced that it has to be like that? Or is it a learned rule that is used, whether or not it is appropriate?

Today Is Not Going So Well, Tomorrow Will Be Better
Source: my own finding

Helps me to get rid of problems and setbacks quicker, and to better handle negative feelings.

Background: there are days when you have a few setbacks. Instead of spiralling into negative thoughts because of this, I use this helping thought. I realise then that it is best if I temporise that day a bit (in order to respect my boundaries). It helps me get rid of negative feelings about this much quicker (instead of endless worrying). I realise that this only says something about that one day when it was not going so well, and that I should not take this personally (I always have setbacks, I can never do anything right, I am in a negative period again…).

First Things First
Source: relaxation therapist

Helps me to plan better and stress less. It also helps me separate the main issues from the side issues.

Background: I have a lot of trouble planning things well and assessing the right amount of time for this. For everything I do, I need more time than I initially thought, which means that I always have to hurry or that I am sometimes late. I am also much slower than others. This helping thought is mostly important for small, more basic planning. With this, the order of planning is adjusted more realistically: instead of beginning with things I think I can do within the available time, I now first start with things that are important for the remainder of that day.

I Am Me
Source: my own finding/books

Helps me to be less perfectionistic and allows me to be myself more.

Background: before the diagnosis of ASD, I was not aware of where my being and thinking different came from. I subconsciously tried to present a neurotypical image of myself to the outside world as much as I could. This image was created based on the high standards I set for myself. In order to answer to that neurotypical image, I consciously and subconsciously used several coping strategies. My weak or less pretty sides were concealed, which eventually caused me to never really dare to be myself. Since the diagnosis and the knowledge I gained from it, I now dare to be myself a lot more. I can accept myself as I am much better now, with my good and my not so good sides. I am me, and others have to take me as I am now.

The Others Are Not Like Me
Source: my own finding

Helps me to learn to understand others better on the one hand (changing of perspective) and to better clarify myself towards others on the other hand.

Background: the power of this helping thought is in the inversion. Instead of 'I am not like the others', I here intentionally use 'the others are not like me'. The perspective is moved. With 'I am not like the others', the perspective comes from the other who sees that you are different. With 'the others are not like me', the perspective comes from within myself. I look at the others and I see that they are not the way I think they should be. I realise that it has mostly to do with my autism (different way of processing information), and I try to put myself more in the place and context of the others. This also works the other way around. The others cannot know what I think and feel, and why I do what I do. When I think there is a difference that might be important for someone else to know in order to understand me better, I try to clarify this more and better.

Other helping thought (list is incomplete)
Children make mistakes
Without failure, no success
Thankfully, there is still work left for tomorrow
Sometimes you win, sometimes you lose
Love it, leave it or change it
Let it go
Stop
Zen
Everything will be okay
We all have our crosses to bear
I don't have to be perfect today
Feel
I'm going for it and I'll see what happens
I'm calm, completely calm
How are we going to deal with that/how are you going to deal with that

Glossary

ADOS-2 A standardised observational instrument used for research on communication, social interaction and (imaginative) play. It can be used when an autism spectrum disorder is suspected.

Asperger's Syndrome developmental disorder as defined in DSM-IV, characterised by impairments in social interactions and a limited repertoire of interests and activities. Separated from the classical autistic disorder in DSM-IV, because there are no deficient language skills in childhood with Asperger's syndrome. Since DSM-5, Asperger's Syndrome is part of the category Autism Spectrum Disorder.

Attention Deficit Hyperactivity Disorder (ADHD) also known as attention deficit hyperkinetic disorder, as defined in DSM-5. Characteristics are impulsive behaviour, concentration problems, restlessness and learning disabilities.

Borderline Personality Disorder emotionally unstable disorder, as defined in DSM-5. Abnormal behaviour, characterised by unstable interpersonal functioning, unstable self-image and heavy mood swings.

Complex figure of Rey-Osterreith neuropsychological assessment. Assessees are asked to reproduce a drawing of a complex figure from an example. After ten minutes they are asked to reproduce it again, this time from memory.

Context blindness trouble with using the context when giving meaning to something.[2]

Diagnostic and Statistical Manual of Mental Disorders (DSM) standard classification of mental disorders, published and produced by the American Psychiatric Association (APA). The current edition is DSM-5.

Deficient Central Coherence the tendency to perceive the world in fragments and having troubles seeing a whole. According to some authors, this is the underlying explanatory model for autistic behaviour.

Executive Functions cognitive processes that enable us to plan ahead and to purposefully solve issues.

Highly Sensitive Personality (HSP) personality type that is more than average stimulated by sensorial stimuli and other experiences.

Intense World Theory localises the origin of autistic behaviour in neurobiology: assumes that people are unable to process sensorial input because of hyperfunctioning local neural microcircuits. Developed by Henry and Kamila Markram.

Interpretative Phenomenological Analysis a type of qualitative research that aims to provide insight in how a specific person, in a specific context, gives meaning to a certain phenomenon.

Minnesota Multiphasic Personality Inventory (MMPI) a standardised psychometric test that tries to map the person's personality and possible personality disorders.

Multiple Complex Developmental Disorder (MCDD) a developmental disorder that used to be classified as PDD-NOS. Characterised by problems with regulating emotions and thoughts, and often psychotic symptoms. Is now categorised as part of the autism spectrum.

Neurodiversity the belief that different neurologic functioning – such as autism – is not necessarily pathologic, but rather a natural version of functioning normally.

Neurotypical people who have an average neurological and psychological development of the brain, as opposed to those who are 'neurodiverse'.

Non-Verbal Learning Disorder neuropsychological diagnosis that mostly causes problems in the nonverbal area. For instance, spatial awareness.

[2] Vermeulen (2009).

Obsessive-Compulsive Disorder disorder as defined in DSM-5, characterised by obsessions (thoughts) and compulsions (actions), that cause suffering and dysfunctioning.

Pervasive Developmental Disorder – Not Otherwise Specified (PDD-NOS) in DSM-IV a rest group for developmental disorders that meet the criteria for pervasive developmental disorders, but not enough characteristics of a specific pervasive developmental disorder. Categorised under Autism Spectrum Disorder Since DSM-5.

Phenomenology philosophical movement, originated in the late nineteenth and early twentieth centuries. Tries to deduct essential characteristics from direct and intuitive experiences, irrespective of presuppositions. In qualitative research, the phenomenological method is primarily focused on describing the experience of a certain phenomenon.

Qualitative Research empirical research which is descriptive in nature and looks for interpretations, experiences and meaning. As opposed to quantitative research, which looks for universal truths that can be expressed in figures, qualitative results are mostly represented in words.

Reading the Mind in the Eye test the subject must try to determine the underlying emotion of a person by looking at pictures of the photographed person's eyes. Developed in 1997 by Simon Baron-Cohen and colleagues to measure the Theory of Mind in adults.

Sally-Anne test neuropsychological test aimed at studying children's are ability to be empathetic towards other people's thoughts. Originally designed by Wimmer and Perner (1983) and later further developed by Uta Frith.

Schizotypal Personality Disorder (STPD) a personality disorder, as defined in DSM-5, with a pervasive pattern of social and interpersonal deficiencies. Feelings of extreme discomfort with having close relationships because of, amongst other things, paranoid ideation. Other characteristics include social anxiety, thought disorder, eccentric behaviour.

Social Responsiveness Scale (SRS) a screening instrument used to map social disabilities with autism spectrum disorders.

Strange Stories (Happé) test that measures Theory of Mind, someone's ability to assess other people's thoughts and feelings.

Theory of Mind the ability to get an idea of someone else's perspective, and the awareness that your own ideas, desires and emotions can diverge from someone else's. A deficient Theory of Mind has often been postulated as the core problem of autism, although this idea has also been criticised. Many people with autism actually *do* develop a Theory of Mind, albeit later than usual. A deficient Theory of Mind is often also connected to a deficient ability to empathise. It should be noted here that the thesis that autistic people have deficient empathic abilities is contested.

Theory of Own Mind the ability to be aware of your own psychological 'self'.

Bibliography

American Psychiatric Association. 2013. *Diagnostic and Statistical Manual of Mental Disorders*. 5th ed. Arlington: American Psychiatric Publishing.

Bargiela, S., R. Steward, and W. Mandy. 2016. The Experiences of Late-Diagnosed Women with Autism Spectrum Conditions: An Investigation of the Female Autism Phenotype. *Journal of Autism and Developmental Disorders* 46 (10): 3281–3294. Springer.

Baron-Cohen, Simon. 1997. *Mindblindness: An Essay on Autism and Theory of Mind*. Cambridge, MA: MIT Press.

Baron-Cohen, S., A.M. Leslie, and U. Frith. 1985. Does the Autistic Child Have a 'Theory of Mind. *Cognition* 21 (1): 37–46. Elsevier, October.

Beardon, Luke. 2017. *Autism and Asperger Syndrome in Adults*. London: Sheldon Press.

Bettelheim, Bruno. 1972. *The Empty Fortress: Infantile Autism and the Birth of the Self*. New edition edition. S.l. New York: Free Press.

Beyers, Leo. 2014. *Het wordende denken*. Antwerp: Maklu.

Dilthey, Wilhelm. 1990. Ideen Über Eine Beschreibende Und Zergliedernde Psychologie (1894). In: *Die Geistige Welt*, 139–240. Gesammelte Schriften, Vol. 5. Vandenhoeck & Ruprecht.

———. 1992. Entwürfe Zur Kritik Der Historischen Vernunft Erster Teil: Erleben, Ausdruck Und Verstehen. In: *Der Aufbau Der Geschichtlichen Welt in Den Geisteswissenschaften*, 191–251. Gesammelte Schriften 7. Vandenhoeck & Ruprecht.

Eyal, Gil, ed. 2010. *The Autism Matrix: The Social Origins of the Autism Epidemic*. Cambridge/Malden, MA: Polity.

Fletcher-Watson, Sue, Fabio Apicella, Bonnie Auyeung, Stepanka Beranova, Frederique Bonnet-Brilhault, Ricardo Canal-Bedia, Tony Charman, et al. 2017. Attitudes of the Autism Community to Early Autism Research. *Autism* 21 (1): 61–74. Sage journals.
Frith, Uta. 2003. *Autism: Explaining the Enigma*. 2nd ed. Malden: Blackwell Pub.
Frith, U., and F. Happé. 1999. Theory of Mind and Self-Consciousness: What Is It Like to Be Autistic? *Mind and Language* 14 (1): 1–22. Wiley.
Gadamer, Hans-Georg. 2014. *Waarheid en methode: hoofdlijnen van een filosofische hermeneutiek*. Nijmegen: Uitgeverij Vantilt.
Goffman, Erving. 1963. *Stigma. Notes on the Management of Spoiled Identity*. Englewood Cliffs: Prentice Hall.
———. 1990. In *Asylums: Essays on the Social Situation of Mental Patients and Other Inmates*, ed. Anchor Books, 1st ed. New York: Anchor Books.
Hacking, Ian. 1996. The Looping Effects of Human Kinds. In *Causal Cognition*, ed. Dan Sperber, David Premack, and Ann James Premack, 351–383. New York: Oxford University Press.
———. 2009a. How We Have Been Learning to Talk About Autism: A Role for Stories. *Metaphilosophy* 40 (3–4): 499–516. Wiley-Blackwell.
———. 2009b. Humans, Aliens & Autism. *Daedalus* 138 (3): 44–59. MIT Press.
Hens, Kristien, Hilde Peeters, and Kris Dierickx. 2016. The Ethics of Complexity. Genetics and Autism, a Literature Review. *American Journal of Medical Genetics Part B: Neuropsychiatric Genetics* 171(B) (3): 305–316. Wiley-Blackwell.
Huws, J.C., and R.S.P. Jones. 2008. Diagnosis, Disclosure, and Having Autism: An Interpretative Phenomenological Analysis of the Perceptions of Young People with Autism. *Journal of Intellectual & Developmental Disability* 33 (2): 99–107. Informa.
Huws, Jaci C., and Robert S.P. Jones. 2015. 'I'm Really Glad This Is Developmental': Autism and Social Comparisons – An Interpretative Phenomenological Analysis. *Autism* 19 (1): 84–90. Sage journals.
Jaarsma, Pier, and Stellan Welin. 2012. Autism as a Natural Human Variation: Reflections on the Claims of the Neurodiversity Movement. *Health Care Analysis* 20 (1): 20–30. Springer.
Jones, R.S.P., A. Zahl, and J.C. Huws. 2001. First-Hand Accounts of Emotional Experiences in Autism: A qualitative analysis. *Disability & Society* 16 (3): 393–401.
Kanner, Leo. 1968. Autistic Disturbances of Affective Contact. *Acta Paedopsychiatrica* 35 (4): 100–136. Schwabe.
Kennett, Jeanette. 2002. Autism, Empathy and Moral Agency. *Philosophical Quarterly* 52 (208): 340–357. Wiley-Blackwell.
Kim, Hyun Uk. 2012. Autism Across Cultures: Rethinking Autism. *Disability & Society* 27 (4): 535–545. Taylor & Francis, June 1.

Kushner, E.S., K.E. Bodner, and N.J. Minshew. 2009. Local vs. Global Approaches to Reproducing the Rey Osterrieth Complex Figure by Children, Adolescents, and Adults with High-Functioning Autism. *Autism Research* 2 (6): 348–358. Wiley-Blackwell, December.

Kusters, Wouter. 2014. *Filosofie van de Waanzin*. Rotterdam: Lemniscaat.

Lester, Jessica. 2012. A Discourse Analysis of Parents' Talk Around Their Children's Autism Labels. *Disability Studies Quarterly* 32 (4). The Ohio State University Libraries. http://dsq-sds.org/article/view/1744/3176.

Magiati, Iliana. 2016. Assessment in Adulthood. In *Handbook of Assessment and Diagnosis of Autism Spectrum Disorder*, ed. Johnny L. Matson, 191–207. Autism and Child Psychopathology Series. Cham: Springer International Publishing.

Markram, H., Tania Rinaldi, and Kamila Markram. 2007. The Intense World Syndrome – An Alternative Hypothesis for Autism. *Frontiers in Neuroscience* 1 (1): 77–96. Frontiers media, October 15.

Masschelein, Anneleen, and Leni Van Goidsenhoven. 2016a. Posting Autism. Online Self-Representation Strategies in Tistje, a Flemish Blog on 'Living on the Spectrum From the Front Row'. In *Disability and Social Media: Global Perspectives*, ed. M. Kent and K. Ellis. London & New York: Ashgate.

———. 2016b. Donna Williams's 'Triumph': Looking for 'the Place in the Middle' at Jessica Kingsley Publishers. *Life Writing* 13 (2): 1–23. Taylor & Francis.

McGeer, Victoria. 2004. Autistic Self-Awareness: Comment. *Philosophy, Psychiatry, and Psychology. Special Issue* 11 (3): 235–251. Johns Hopkins University Press.

———. 2008. Varieties of Moral Agency: Lessons From Autism (and Psychopathy). In *Moral Psychology*, ed. Walter Sinnott-Armstrong, vol. 3. Cambridge, MA: MIT Press.

Milton, Damian. 2017. *A Mismatch of Salience*. Hove: Pavilion Publishing.

Murray, Stuart. 2008. *Representing Autism: Culture, Narrative, Fascination*. Liverpool: Liverpool University Press.

Nadesan, Majia Holmer. 2005. *Constructing Autism: Unravelling the "Truth" and Understanding the Social*. London/New York: Routledge.

Nicolaidis, Christina, Dora M. Raymaker, Elesia Ashkenazy, Katherine E. McDonald, Sebastian Dern, Amelia E.V. Baggs, Steven K. Kapp, Michael Weiner, and W. Cody Boisclair. 2015. 'Respect the Way I Need to Communicate with You': Healthcare Experiences of Adults on the Autism Spectrum. *Autism* 19 (7): 824–831. Sage Journals, October 1.

Pellicano, Elizabeth, and Marc Stears. 2011. Bridging Autism, Science and Society: Moving Toward an Ethically Informed Approach to Autism Research. *Autism Research: Official Journal of the International Society for Autism Research* 4 (4): 271–282. INSAR, August.

Pellicano, Elizabeth, Adam Dinsmore, and Tony Charman. 2014. What Should Autism Research Focus Upon? Community Views and Priorities from the United Kingdom. *Autism* 18 (7): 756–770. Sage Journals, October.

Pentzell, Nick. 2013. I Think, Therefore I Am. I Am Verbal, Therefore I Live. In *The Philosophy of Autism*, ed. Jami L. Anderson and Simon Cushing, 103–108. Lanham: Rowman & Littlefield.

Prince-Hughes, Dawn. 2002. *Aquamarine Blue 5*. Athens: Swallow Press.

Robertson, A.E., and David R. Simmons. 2015. The Sensory Experiences of Adults with Autism Spectrum Disorder: A Qualitative Analysis. *Perception* 44 (5): 569–586. Sage Journals.

Rorty, Richard. 1980. *Philosophy and the Mirror of Nature*. Princeton: Princeton University Press.

Schriber, Roberta A., Richard W. Robins, and Marjorie Solomon. 2014. Personality and Self-Insight in Individuals with Autism Spectrum Disorder. *Journal of Personality and Social Psychology* 106 (1): 112–130. American Psychological Association.

Singh, Jennifer S. 2016. Parenting Work and Autism Trajectories of Care. *Sociology of Health & Illness* 38 (7): 1106–1120. Wiley.

Smith, Jonathan. 2009. *Interpretative Phenomenological Analysis: Theory, Method and Research*. 1st ed. Los Angeles: Sage.

Spek, Annelies. http://www.anneliesspek.nl/pagina27.html. Visited: 08/05/2017.

Thienpont, Lieve. 2017. *De pijn van anders zijn*. Gent: Academia Press.

Trembath, D., C. Germano, G. Johanson, and C. Dissanayake. 2012. The Experience of Anxiety in Young Adults With Autism Spectrum Disorders. *Focus on Autism and Other Developmental Disabilities* 27 (4): 213–224. Sage Publications.

Van de Cruys, Kris Evers Sander, Ruth Van der Hallen, Lien Van Eylen, Bart Boets, Lee de-Wit, and Johan Wagemans. 2014. Precise Minds in Uncertain Worlds: Predictive Coding in Autism. *Psychological Review* 121 (4): 649–675. American Psychological Association, October.

Van Goidsenhoven, Leni. 2017. How to Think About 'Autie-Biographies'? Life Writing Genres and Strategies from an Autistic Perspective. *Language, Literature and Culture* 64 (2): 1–17.

Van Manen, Max. 1990. *Researching Lived Experience: Human Science for an Action Sensitive Pedagogy*. 2nd ed. Albany: State University of New York Press.

———. 2014. *Phenomenology of Practice: Meaning-Giving Methods in Phenomenological Research and Writing*. Walnut Creek: Routledge.

Verhoeff, Berend. 2013a. Autism in Flux: A History of the Concept from Leo Kanner to DSM-5. *History of Psychiatry* 24 (4): 442–458. Sage Publications, December 1.

———. 2013b. The Autism Puzzle: Challenging a Mechanistic Model on Conceptual and Historical Grounds. *Philosophy, Ethics, and Humanities in Medicine* 8 (1): 17. Springer.

———. 2015. Fundamental Challenges for Autism Research: The Science-Practice Gap, Demarcating Autism and the Unsuccessful Search for the Neurobiological Basis of Autism. *Medicine, Health Care, and Philosophy* 18 (3): 443–447. Springer, August.

Vermeulen, Peter. 2009. *Autisme Als Contextblindheid*. Leuven: Acco.

Waltz, Mitzi. 2013. *Autism. A Social and Medical History*. Hampshire: Palgrave Macmillan.

Waterhouse, Lynn. 2013. *Rethinking Autism: Variation and Complexity*. London/Waltham, MA: Academic.

Wiorkowski, F. 2015. The Experiences of Students with Autism Spectrum Disorders in College: A Heuristic Exploration. *The Qualitative Report* 20 (6): 847. Nova Southeastern University.

Yusuf, Afiqah, and Mayada Elsabbagh. 2015. At the Cross-Roads of Participatory Research and Biomarker Discovery in Autism: The Need for Empirical Data. *BMC Medical Ethics* 16: 88.

Index[1]

A
ADOS-2, *see* Autism Diagnostic Observation Scale
Alexithymia, 101
Asperger's syndrome, 23, 46, 48, 52, 80, 82, 83, 122
Attention Deficit Hyperactivity Disorder (ADHD), 71, 82, 84
Autism coach, 121–123
Autism Diagnostic Observation Scale (ADOS-2), 63, 64, 68
Autism spectrum disorder (ASD), 4, 5, 9, 11, 12, 24, 25, 28, 46, 48, 63, 68, 69, 73, 80, 82, 83, 89, 109, 113, 121, 123, 137, 141

B
Baron-Cohen, Simon, 6n14, 66
Bettelheim, Bruno, 5
Borderline, 70, 84, 113
Borderline personality disorder, 48, 56, 82, 83, 134

C
Central coherence, 7, 8, 64, 68, 69, 96
Common variants, 6
Communication Analysis, 2, 3
Complex figure of Rey, 63, 64, 69
Context blindness, 7, 110, 137
Context sensitivity, 77

D
Depression, 40, 45, 46, 48, 54, 56–58, 84, 85, 93, 101, 115, 122
Dilthey, Wilhelm, 97, 130
DSM-IV, 4, 82
DSM-5, 4, 7, 34, 37, 46, 69, 73, 83, 133

E
Embryo selection, 2
Empathy, 31, 32, 75, 109
Epilepsy, 48

[1] Note: Page numbers followed by 'n' refer to notes.

Euthanasia, 56–58
Exculpating, 81
Executive functions, 7, 8, 63–65, 68, 69, 96
Eyal, Gil, 9

F
Flemish Autism Association (*Vlaamse Vereniging Autisme*), 12, 48, 124
Fragile-X, 5
Frith, Uta, 6n14, 7n15, 22, 96

G
Gadamer, Hans-Georg, 134
Generalised anxiety disorder, 48

H
Helping thoughts, 93, 137–142
High, Inflexible Precision of Prediction Errors in Autism (HIPPEA), 7, 131
High Sensitive Person (HSP), 72, 83
High Sensitive Personality, 72
High sensitivity, 71, 72, 83
HIPPEA, *see* High, Inflexible Precision of Prediction Errors in Autism
HSP, *see* High Sensitive Person

I
Intense World Theory, 7, 131
Interpretative Phenomenological Analysis (IPA), 11, 12
IQ, 4, 12, 13, 63, 72, 130

J
Justice, 36, 98

K
Kanner, Leo, 4, 9

L
Lester, Jessica, 106
Loneliness, 53, 54, 59
Looping effect, 9, 133

M
Minnesota Multiphasic Personality Inventory (MMPI), 70
MMPI, *see* Minnesota Multiphasic Personality Inventory
Moral career, 133
Murray, Stuart, 9

N
Neurodiversity, 5
NLD, *see* Non-verbal learning disorder
Non-verbal learning disorder (NLD), 24, 36, 48, 72, 73, 125, 134

O
Obsessive Compulsive Personality Disorder (OCPD), 72, 83

P
PDD-NOS, *see* Pervasive Developmental Disorder—Not Otherwise Specified
Pentzell, Nick, 8
Pervasive Developmental Disorder—Not Otherwise Specified (PDD-NOS), 4
Phenomenological, 11
Prenatal diagnosis, 2

R
Reading the Mind in the Eye test, 66, 74
Responsibility, 113
Rorty, Richard, 134

S
Schizotypal personality disorder, 48
Singh, Jennifer, 106
Social Responsiveness Scale (SRS), 68, 75
Stigma, 133
Strange Stories, 66
Suicide, 45, 47, 57, 58, 85
Sympathy, 32

T
Theory of Mind (ToM), 6, 8, 12, 63, 64, 66, 68, 69, 96, 110
Theory of Own Mind, 7
Tower of London Test, 65

V
Van de Cruys, Sander, 7
Verhoeff, Berend, 9

W
Waltz, Mitzi, 7
Weak central coherence, 8, 69, 110
Wisconsin Card Sorting Test, 63, 65

Printed in the United States
By Bookmasters